ISBN 0-8373-3383-0
C-3383   CAREER EXAMINATION SERIES

This is your PASSBOOK® for...

Bus Operator/Conductor

Test Preparation Study Guide

Questions & Answers

NATIONAL LEARNING CORPORATION

Copyright © 2017 by

National Learning Corporation

212 Michael Drive, Syosset, New York 11791

All rights reserved, including the right of reproduction in whole or in part, in any form or by any means, electronic or mechanical, including photocopying, recording, or by any information storage and retrieval system, without permission in writing from the Publisher.

(516) 921-8888
(800) 632-8888
(800) 645-6337
FAX: (516) 921-8743
www.passbooks.com
info @ passbooks.com

PRINTED IN THE UNITED STATES OF AMERICA

PASSBOOK®
NOTICE

This book is SOLELY intended for, is sold ONLY to, and its use is RESTRICTED to *individual*, bona fide applicants or candidates who qualify by virtue of having seriously filed applications for appropriate license, certificate, professional and/or promotional advancement, higher school matriculation, scholarship, or other legitimate requirements of educational and/or governmental authorities.

This book is NOT intended for use, class instruction, tutoring, training, duplication, copying, reprinting, excerption, or adaptation, etc., by:

(1) Other publishers

(2) Proprietors and/or Instructors of "Coaching" and/or Preparatory Courses

(3) Personnel and/or Training Divisions of commercial, industrial, and governmental organizations

(4) Schools, colleges, or universities and/or their departments and staffs, including teachers and other personnel

(5) Testing Agencies or Bureaus

(6) Study groups which seek by the purchase of a single volume to copy and/or duplicate and/or adapt this material for use by the group as a whole without having purchased individual volumes for each of the members of the group

(7) Et al.

Such persons would be in violation of appropriate Federal and State statutes.

PROVISION OF LICENSING AGREEMENTS. — Recognized educational commercial, industrial, and governmental institutions and organizations, and others legitimately engaged in educational pursuits, including training, testing, and measurement activities, may address a request for a licensing agreement to the copyright owners, who will determine whether, and under what conditions, including fees and charges, the materials in this book may be used by them. In other words, a licensing facility exists for the legitimate use of the material in this book on other than an individual basis. However, it is asseverated and affirmed here that the material in this book *CANNOT* be used without the receipt of the express permission of such a licensing agreement from the Publishers.

NATIONAL LEARNING CORPORATION
212 Michael Drive
Syosset, New York 11791

Inquiries re licensing agreements should be addressed to:
The President
National Learning Corporation
212 Michael Drive
Syosset, New York 11791

PASSBOOK® SERIES

THE *PASSBOOK® SERIES* has been created to prepare applicants and candidates for the ultimate academic battlefield – the examination room.

At some time in our lives, each and every one of us may be required to take an examination – for validation, matriculation, admission, qualification, registration, certification, or licensure.

Based on the assumption that every applicant or candidate has met the basic formal educational standards, has taken the required number of courses, and read the necessary texts, the *PASSBOOK® SERIES* furnishes the one special preparation which may assure passing with confidence, instead of failing with insecurity. Examination questions – together with answers – are furnished as the basic vehicle for study so that the mysteries of the examination and its compounding difficulties may be eliminated or diminished by a sure method.

This book is meant to help you pass your examination provided that you qualify and are serious in your objective.

The entire field is reviewed through the huge store of content information which is succinctly presented through a provocative and challenging approach – the question-and-answer method.

A climate of success is established by furnishing the correct answers at the end of each test.

You soon learn to recognize types of questions, forms of questions, and patterns of questioning. You may even begin to anticipate expected outcomes.

You perceive that many questions are repeated or adapted so that you can gain acute insights, which may enable you to score many sure points.

You learn how to confront new questions, or types of questions, and to attack them confidently and work out the correct answers.

You note objectives and emphases, and recognize pitfalls and dangers, so that you may make positive educational adjustments.

Moreover, you are kept fully informed in relation to new concepts, methods, practices, and directions in the field.

You discover that you are actually taking the examination all the time: you are preparing for the examination by "taking" an examination, not by reading extraneous and/or supererogatory textbooks.

In short, this PASSBOOK®, used directedly, should be an important factor in helping you to pass your test.

BUS OPERATOR/CONDUCTOR

DUTIES AND RESPONSIBILITIES

As a Bus Operator, operates a bus in accordance with the rules and regulations of the transit authority. Performs such other duties as the transit authority is authorized by law to prescribe in its regulations.

As a Conductor, is immediately responsible for the safety, regularity and proper care of trains, in accordance with the transit authority rules, regulations and special instructions. May be assigned to work as a passenger train conductor, a platform conductor or a yard conductor.

EXAMPIES OF TYPICAL TASKS:

As a Bus Operator: In addition to driving the bus; collect fares; issues and collects transfers; looks out for the safety of the passengers; protects the assigned vehicle; writes reports concerning revenues, accidents, faulty equipment and unusual occurrences.

As a Conductor: When assigned to a train: takes charge of train; checks route and destination signs; checks for breakage or defects in any of the cars; safely opens and closes car doors; makes announcements to passengers over the public address system. When assigned to a station platform: oversees the safe movement of passenger off and on trains; assists in the safe dispatch of trains; watches exits gates and patrols station platform. When assigned to a yard: operates hand throw switches; assists in making coupling; serves as flagmen.

SCOPE OF THE WRITTEN TEST

The written test will be of the multiple-choice type and may include questions on: dealing effectively with the public; rules of the road and safe driving techniques; reading and interpreting relevant written material; bulletins; reading and interpreting transit schedules and route maps; the locations of major points of interest and other related areas.

HOW TO TAKE A TEST

I. YOU MUST PASS AN EXAMINATION

A. *WHAT EVERY CANDIDATE SHOULD KNOW*

Examination applicants often ask us for help in preparing for the written test. What can I study in advance? What kinds of questions will be asked? How will the test be given? How will the papers be graded?

As an applicant for a civil service examination, you may be wondering about some of these things. Our purpose here is to suggest effective methods of advance study and to describe civil service examinations.

Your chances for success on this examination can be increased if you know how to prepare. Those "pre-examination jitters" can be reduced if you know what to expect. You can even experience an adventure in good citizenship if you know why civil service exams are given.

B. *WHY ARE CIVIL SERVICE EXAMINATIONS GIVEN?*

Civil service examinations are important to you in two ways. As a citizen, you want public jobs filled by employees who know how to do their work. As a job seeker, you want a fair chance to compete for that job on an equal footing with other candidates. The best-known means of accomplishing this two-fold goal is the competitive examination.

Exams are widely publicized throughout the nation. They may be administered for jobs in federal, state, city, municipal, town or village governments or agencies.

Any citizen may apply, with some limitations, such as the age or residence of applicants. Your experience and education may be reviewed to see whether you meet the requirements for the particular examination. When these requirements exist, they are reasonable and applied consistently to all applicants. Thus, a competitive examination may cause you some uneasiness now, but it is your privilege and safeguard.

C. *HOW ARE CIVIL SERVICE EXAMS DEVELOPED?*

Examinations are carefully written by trained technicians who are specialists in the field known as "psychological measurement," in consultation with recognized authorities in the field of work that the test will cover. These experts recommend the subject matter areas or skills to be tested; only those knowledges or skills important to your success on the job are included. The most reliable books and source materials available are used as references. Together, the experts and technicians judge the difficulty level of the questions.

Test technicians know how to phrase questions so that the problem is clearly stated. Their ethics do not permit "trick" or "catch" questions. Questions may have been tried out on sample groups, or subjected to statistical analysis, to determine their usefulness.

Written tests are often used in combination with performance tests, ratings of training and experience, and oral interviews. All of these measures combine to form the best-known means of finding the right person for the right job.

II. HOW TO PASS THE WRITTEN TEST

A. NATURE OF THE EXAMINATION

To prepare intelligently for civil service examinations, you should know how they differ from school examinations you have taken. In school you were assigned certain definite pages to read or subjects to cover. The examination questions were quite detailed and usually emphasized memory. Civil service exams, on the other hand, try to discover your present ability to perform the duties of a position, plus your potentiality to learn these duties. In other words, a civil service exam attempts to predict how successful you will be. Questions cover such a broad area that they cannot be as minute and detailed as school exam questions.

In the public service similar kinds of work, or positions, are grouped together in one "class." This process is known as *position-classification*. All the positions in a class are paid according to the salary range for that class. One class title covers all of these positions, and they are all tested by the same examination.

B. FOUR BASIC STEPS

1) Study the announcement

How, then, can you know what subjects to study? Our best answer is: "Learn as much as possible about the class of positions for which you've applied." The exam will test the knowledge, skills and abilities needed to do the work.

Your most valuable source of information about the position you want is the official exam announcement. This announcement lists the training and experience qualifications. Check these standards and apply only if you come reasonably close to meeting them.

The brief description of the position in the examination announcement offers some clues to the subjects which will be tested. Think about the job itself. Review the duties in your mind. Can you perform them, or are there some in which you are rusty? Fill in the blank spots in your preparation.

Many jurisdictions preview the written test in the exam announcement by including a section called "Knowledge and Abilities Required," "Scope of the Examination," or some similar heading. Here you will find out specifically what fields will be tested.

2) Review your own background

Once you learn in general what the position is all about, and what you need to know to do the work, ask yourself which subjects you already know fairly well and which need improvement. You may wonder whether to concentrate on improving your strong areas or on building some background in your fields of weakness. When the announcement has specified "some knowledge" or "considerable knowledge," or has used adjectives like "beginning principles of…" or "advanced … methods," you can get a clue as to the number and difficulty of questions to be asked in any given field. More questions, and hence broader coverage, would be included for those subjects which are more important in the work. Now weigh your strengths and weaknesses against the job requirements and prepare accordingly.

3) Determine the level of the position

Another way to tell how intensively you should prepare is to understand the level of the job for which you are applying. Is it the entering level? In other words, is this the position in which beginners in a field of work are hired? Or is it an intermediate or advanced level? Sometimes this is indicated by such words as "Junior" or "Senior" in the class title. Other jurisdictions use Roman numerals to designate the level – Clerk I, Clerk II, for example. The word "Supervisor" sometimes appears in the title. If the level is not indicated by the title, check the description of duties. Will you be working under very close supervision, or will you have responsibility for independent decisions in this work?

4) Choose appropriate study materials

Now that you know the subjects to be examined and the relative amount of each subject to be covered, you can choose suitable study materials. For beginning level jobs, or even advanced ones, if you have a pronounced weakness in some aspect of your training, read a modern, standard textbook in that field. Be sure it is up to date and has general coverage. Such books are normally available at your library, and the librarian will be glad to help you locate one. For entry-level positions, questions of appropriate difficulty are chosen – neither highly advanced questions, nor those too simple. Such questions require careful thought but not advanced training.

If the position for which you are applying is technical or advanced, you will read more advanced, specialized material. If you are already familiar with the basic principles of your field, elementary textbooks would waste your time. Concentrate on advanced textbooks and technical periodicals. Think through the concepts and review difficult problems in your field.

These are all general sources. You can get more ideas on your own initiative, following these leads. For example, training manuals and publications of the government agency which employs workers in your field can be useful, particularly for technical and professional positions. A letter or visit to the government department involved may result in more specific study suggestions, and certainly will provide you with a more definite idea of the exact nature of the position you are seeking.

III. KINDS OF TESTS

Tests are used for purposes other than measuring knowledge and ability to perform specified duties. For some positions, it is equally important to test ability to make adjustments to new situations or to profit from training. In others, basic mental abilities not dependent on information are essential. Questions which test these things may not appear as pertinent to the duties of the position as those which test for knowledge and information. Yet they are often highly important parts of a fair examination. For very general questions, it is almost impossible to help you direct your study efforts. What we can do is to point out some of the more common of these general abilities needed in public service positions and describe some typical questions.

1) General information

Broad, general information has been found useful for predicting job success in some kinds of work. This is tested in a variety of ways, from vocabulary lists to questions about current events. Basic background in some field of work, such as sociology or economics, may be sampled in a group of questions. Often these are principles which have become familiar to most persons through exposure rather than through formal training. It is difficult to advise you how to study for these questions; being alert to the world around you is our best suggestion.

2) Verbal ability

An example of an ability needed in many positions is verbal or language ability. Verbal ability is, in brief, the ability to use and understand words. Vocabulary and grammar tests are typical measures of this ability. Reading comprehension or paragraph interpretation questions are common in many kinds of civil service tests. You are given a paragraph of written material and asked to find its central meaning.

3) Numerical ability
Number skills can be tested by the familiar arithmetic problem, by checking paired lists of numbers to see which are alike and which are different, or by interpreting charts and graphs. In the latter test, a graph may be printed in the test booklet which you are asked to use as the basis for answering questions.

4) Observation
A popular test for law-enforcement positions is the observation test. A picture is shown to you for several minutes, then taken away. Questions about the picture test your ability to observe both details and larger elements.

5) Following directions
In many positions in the public service, the employee must be able to carry out written instructions dependably and accurately. You may be given a chart with several columns, each column listing a variety of information. The questions require you to carry out directions involving the information given in the chart.

6) Skills and aptitudes
Performance tests effectively measure some manual skills and aptitudes. When the skill is one in which you are trained, such as typing or shorthand, you can practice. These tests are often very much like those given in business school or high school courses. For many of the other skills and aptitudes, however, no short-time preparation can be made. Skills and abilities natural to you or that you have developed throughout your lifetime are being tested.

Many of the general questions just described provide all the data needed to answer the questions and ask you to use your reasoning ability to find the answers. Your best preparation for these tests, as well as for tests of facts and ideas, is to be at your physical and mental best. You, no doubt, have your own methods of getting into an exam-taking mood and keeping "in shape." The next section lists some ideas on this subject.

IV. KINDS OF QUESTIONS

Only rarely is the "essay" question, which you answer in narrative form, used in civil service tests. Civil service tests are usually of the short-answer type. Full instructions for answering these questions will be given to you at the examination. But in case this is your first experience with short-answer questions and separate answer sheets, here is what you need to know:

1) Multiple-choice Questions
Most popular of the short-answer questions is the "multiple choice" or "best answer" question. It can be used, for example, to test for factual knowledge, ability to solve problems or judgment in meeting situations found at work.
A multiple-choice question is normally one of three types—
- It can begin with an incomplete statement followed by several possible endings. You are to find the one ending which *best* completes the statement, although some of the others may not be entirely wrong.
- It can also be a complete statement in the form of a question which is answered by choosing one of the statements listed.

- It can be in the form of a problem – again you select the best answer.

Here is an example of a multiple-choice question with a discussion which should give you some clues as to the method for choosing the right answer:

When an employee has a complaint about his assignment, the action which will *best* help him overcome his difficulty is to
    A. discuss his difficulty with his coworkers
    B. take the problem to the head of the organization
    C. take the problem to the person who gave him the assignment
    D. say nothing to anyone about his complaint

In answering this question, you should study each of the choices to find which is best. Consider choice "A" – Certainly an employee may discuss his complaint with fellow employees, but no change or improvement can result, and the complaint remains unresolved. Choice "B" is a poor choice since the head of the organization probably does not know what assignment you have been given, and taking your problem to him is known as "going over the head" of the supervisor. The supervisor, or person who made the assignment, is the person who can clarify it or correct any injustice. Choice "C" is, therefore, correct. To say nothing, as in choice "D," is unwise. Supervisors have and interest in knowing the problems employees are facing, and the employee is seeking a solution to his problem.

2) True/False Questions

The "true/false" or "right/wrong" form of question is sometimes used. Here a complete statement is given. Your job is to decide whether the statement is right or wrong.

SAMPLE: A roaming cell-phone call to a nearby city costs less than a non-roaming call to a distant city.

This statement is wrong, or false, since roaming calls are more expensive.

This is not a complete list of all possible question forms, although most of the others are variations of these common types. You will always get complete directions for answering questions. Be sure you understand *how* to mark your answers – ask questions until you do.

V. RECORDING YOUR ANSWERS

Computer terminals are used more and more today for many different kinds of exams.

For an examination with very few applicants, you may be told to record your answers in the test booklet itself. Separate answer sheets are much more common. If this separate answer sheet is to be scored by machine – and this is often the case – it is highly important that you mark your answers correctly in order to get credit.

An electronic scoring machine is often used in civil service offices because of the speed with which papers can be scored. Machine-scored answer sheets must be marked with a pencil, which will be given to you. This pencil has a high graphite content which responds to the electronic scoring machine. As a matter of fact, stray dots may register as answers, so do not let your pencil rest on the answer sheet while you are pondering the correct answer. Also, if your pencil lead breaks or is otherwise defective, ask for another.

Since the answer sheet will be dropped in a slot in the scoring machine, be careful not to bend the corners or get the paper crumpled.

The answer sheet normally has five vertical columns of numbers, with 30 numbers to a column. These numbers correspond to the question numbers in your test booklet. After each number, going across the page are four or five pairs of dotted lines. These short dotted lines have small letters or numbers above them. The first two pairs may also have a "T" or "F" above the letters. This indicates that the first two pairs only are to be used if the questions are of the true-false type. If the questions are multiple choice, disregard the "T" and "F" and pay attention only to the small letters or numbers.

Answer your questions in the manner of the sample that follows:

32. The largest city in the United States is
    A. Washington, D.C.
    B. New York City
    C. Chicago
    D. Detroit
    E. San Francisco

1) Choose the answer you think is best. (New York City is the largest, so "B" is correct.)
2) Find the row of dotted lines numbered the same as the question you are answering. (Find row number 32)
3) Find the pair of dotted lines corresponding to the answer. (Find the pair of lines under the mark "B.")
4) Make a solid black mark between the dotted lines.

VI. BEFORE THE TEST

Common sense will help you find procedures to follow to get ready for an examination. Too many of us, however, overlook these sensible measures. Indeed, nervousness and fatigue have been found to be the most serious reasons why applicants fail to do their best on civil service tests. Here is a list of reminders:

- Begin your preparation early – Don't wait until the last minute to go scurrying around for books and materials or to find out what the position is all about.
- Prepare continuously – An hour a night for a week is better than an all-night cram session. This has been definitely established. What is more, a night a week for a month will return better dividends than crowding your study into a shorter period of time.
- Locate the place of the exam – You have been sent a notice telling you when and where to report for the examination. If the location is in a different town or otherwise unfamiliar to you, it would be well to inquire the best route and learn something about the building.
- Relax the night before the test – Allow your mind to rest. Do not study at all that night. Plan some mild recreation or diversion; then go to bed early and get a good night's sleep.
- Get up early enough to make a leisurely trip to the place for the test – This way unforeseen events, traffic snarls, unfamiliar buildings, etc. will not upset you.
- Dress comfortably – A written test is not a fashion show. You will be known by number and not by name, so wear something comfortable.

- Leave excess paraphernalia at home – Shopping bags and odd bundles will get in your way. You need bring only the items mentioned in the official notice you received; usually everything you need is provided. Do not bring reference books to the exam. They will only confuse those last minutes and be taken away from you when in the test room.
- Arrive somewhat ahead of time – If because of transportation schedules you must get there very early, bring a newspaper or magazine to take your mind off yourself while waiting.
- Locate the examination room – When you have found the proper room, you will be directed to the seat or part of the room where you will sit. Sometimes you are given a sheet of instructions to read while you are waiting. Do not fill out any forms until you are told to do so; just read them and be prepared.
- Relax and prepare to listen to the instructions
- If you have any physical problem that may keep you from doing your best, be sure to tell the test administrator. If you are sick or in poor health, you really cannot do your best on the exam. You can come back and take the test some other time.

VII. AT THE TEST

The day of the test is here and you have the test booklet in your hand. The temptation to get going is very strong. Caution! There is more to success than knowing the right answers. You must know how to identify your papers and understand variations in the type of short-answer question used in this particular examination. Follow these suggestions for maximum results from your efforts:

1) Cooperate with the monitor

The test administrator has a duty to create a situation in which you can be as much at ease as possible. He will give instructions, tell you when to begin, check to see that you are marking your answer sheet correctly, and so on. He is not there to guard you, although he will see that your competitors do not take unfair advantage. He wants to help you do your best.

2) Listen to all instructions

Don't jump the gun! Wait until you understand all directions. In most civil service tests you get more time than you need to answer the questions. So don't be in a hurry. Read each word of instructions until you clearly understand the meaning. Study the examples, listen to all announcements and follow directions. Ask questions if you do not understand what to do.

3) Identify your papers

Civil service exams are usually identified by number only. You will be assigned a number; you must not put your name on your test papers. Be sure to copy your number correctly. Since more than one exam may be given, copy your exact examination title.

4) Plan your time

Unless you are told that a test is a "speed" or "rate of work" test, speed itself is usually not important. Time enough to answer all the questions will be provided, but this does not mean that you have all day. An overall time limit has been set. Divide the total time (in minutes) by the number of questions to determine the approximate time you have for each question.

5) Do not linger over difficult questions

If you come across a difficult question, mark it with a paper clip (useful to have along) and come back to it when you have been through the booklet. One caution if you do this – be sure to skip a number on your answer sheet as well. Check often to be sure that you have not lost your place and that you are marking in the row numbered the same as the question you are answering.

6) Read the questions

Be sure you know what the question asks! Many capable people are unsuccessful because they failed to *read* the questions correctly.

7) Answer all questions

Unless you have been instructed that a penalty will be deducted for incorrect answers, it is better to guess than to omit a question.

8) Speed tests

It is often better NOT to guess on speed tests. It has been found that on timed tests people are tempted to spend the last few seconds before time is called in marking answers at random – without even reading them – in the hope of picking up a few extra points. To discourage this practice, the instructions may warn you that your score will be "corrected" for guessing. That is, a penalty will be applied. The incorrect answers will be deducted from the correct ones, or some other penalty formula will be used.

9) Review your answers

If you finish before time is called, go back to the questions you guessed or omitted to give them further thought. Review other answers if you have time.

10) Return your test materials

If you are ready to leave before others have finished or time is called, take ALL your materials to the monitor and leave quietly. Never take any test material with you. The monitor can discover whose papers are not complete, and taking a test booklet may be grounds for disqualification.

VIII. EXAMINATION TECHNIQUES

1) Read the general instructions carefully. These are usually printed on the first page of the exam booklet. As a rule, these instructions refer to the timing of the examination; the fact that you should not start work until the signal and must stop work at a signal, etc. If there are any *special* instructions, such as a choice of questions to be answered, make sure that you note this instruction carefully.

2) When you are ready to start work on the examination, that is as soon as the signal has been given, read the instructions to each question booklet, underline any key words or phrases, such as *least, best, outline, describe* and the like. In this way you will tend to answer as requested rather than discover on reviewing your paper that you *listed without describing*, that you selected the *worst* choice rather than the *best* choice, etc.

3) If the examination is of the objective or multiple-choice type – that is, each question will also give a series of possible answers: A, B, C or D, and you are called upon to select the best answer and write the letter next to that answer on your answer paper – it is advisable to start answering each question in turn. There may be anywhere from 50 to 100 such questions in the three or four hours allotted and you can see how much time would be taken if you read through all the questions before beginning to answer any. Furthermore, if you come across a question or group of questions which you know would be difficult to answer, it would undoubtedly affect your handling of all the other questions.

4) If the examination is of the essay type and contains but a few questions, it is a moot point as to whether you should read all the questions before starting to answer any one. Of course, if you are given a choice – say five out of seven and the like – then it is essential to read all the questions so you can eliminate the two that are most difficult. If, however, you are asked to answer all the questions, there may be danger in trying to answer the easiest one first because you may find that you will spend too much time on it. The best technique is to answer the first question, then proceed to the second, etc.

5) Time your answers. Before the exam begins, write down the time it started, then add the time allowed for the examination and write down the time it must be completed, then divide the time available somewhat as follows:
    - If 3-1/2 hours are allowed, that would be 210 minutes. If you have 80 objective-type questions, that would be an average of 2-1/2 minutes per question. Allow yourself no more than 2 minutes per question, or a total of 160 minutes, which will permit about 50 minutes to review.
    - If for the time allotment of 210 minutes there are 7 essay questions to answer, that would average about 30 minutes a question. Give yourself only 25 minutes per question so that you have about 35 minutes to review.

6) The most important instruction is to *read each question* and make sure you know what is wanted. The second most important instruction is to *time yourself properly* so that you answer every question. The third most important instruction is to *answer every question*. Guess if you have to but include something for each question. Remember that you will receive no credit for a blank and will probably receive some credit if you write something in answer to an essay question. If you guess a letter – say "B" for a multiple-choice question – you may have guessed right. If you leave a blank as an answer to a multiple-choice question, the examiners may respect your feelings but it will not add a point to your score. Some exams may penalize you for wrong answers, so in such cases *only*, you may not want to guess unless you have some basis for your answer.

7) Suggestions
   a. Objective-type questions
      1. Examine the question booklet for proper sequence of pages and questions
      2. Read all instructions carefully
      3. Skip any question which seems too difficult; return to it after all other questions have been answered
      4. Apportion your time properly; do not spend too much time on any single question or group of questions

5. Note and underline key words – *all, most, fewest, least, best, worst, same, opposite,* etc.
6. Pay particular attention to negatives
7. Note unusual option, e.g., unduly long, short, complex, different or similar in content to the body of the question
8. Observe the use of "hedging" words – *probably, may, most likely,* etc.
9. Make sure that your answer is put next to the same number as the question
10. Do not second-guess unless you have good reason to believe the second answer is definitely more correct
11. Cross out original answer if you decide another answer is more accurate; do not erase until you are ready to hand your paper in
12. Answer all questions; guess unless instructed otherwise
13. Leave time for review

  b. Essay questions
1. Read each question carefully
2. Determine exactly what is wanted. Underline key words or phrases.
3. Decide on outline or paragraph answer
4. Include many different points and elements unless asked to develop any one or two points or elements
5. Show impartiality by giving pros and cons unless directed to select one side only
6. Make and write down any assumptions you find necessary to answer the questions
7. Watch your English, grammar, punctuation and choice of words
8. Time your answers; don't crowd material

8) Answering the essay question

Most essay questions can be answered by framing the specific response around several key words or ideas. Here are a few such key words or ideas:

M's: manpower, materials, methods, money, management
P's: purpose, program, policy, plan, procedure, practice, problems, pitfalls, personnel, public relations

  a. Six basic steps in handling problems:
1. Preliminary plan and background development
2. Collect information, data and facts
3. Analyze and interpret information, data and facts
4. Analyze and develop solutions as well as make recommendations
5. Prepare report and sell recommendations
6. Install recommendations and follow up effectiveness

  b. Pitfalls to avoid
1. *Taking things for granted* – A statement of the situation does not necessarily imply that each of the elements is necessarily true; for example, a complaint may be invalid and biased so that all that can be taken for granted is that a complaint has been registered

2. *Considering only one side of a situation* – Wherever possible, indicate several alternatives and then point out the reasons you selected the best one
3. *Failing to indicate follow up* – Whenever your answer indicates action on your part, make certain that you will take proper follow-up action to see how successful your recommendations, procedures or actions turn out to be
4. *Taking too long in answering any single question* – Remember to time your answers properly

IX. AFTER THE TEST

Scoring procedures differ in detail among civil service jurisdictions although the general principles are the same. Whether the papers are hand-scored or graded by machine we have described, they are nearly always graded by number. That is, the person who marks the paper knows only the number – never the name – of the applicant. Not until all the papers have been graded will they be matched with names. If other tests, such as training and experience or oral interview ratings have been given, scores will be combined. Different parts of the examination usually have different weights. For example, the written test might count 60 percent of the final grade, and a rating of training and experience 40 percent. In many jurisdictions, veterans will have a certain number of points added to their grades.

After the final grade has been determined, the names are placed in grade order and an eligible list is established. There are various methods for resolving ties between those who get the same final grade – probably the most common is to place first the name of the person whose application was received first. Job offers are made from the eligible list in the order the names appear on it. You will be notified of your grade and your rank as soon as all these computations have been made. This will be done as rapidly as possible.

People who are found to meet the requirements in the announcement are called "eligibles." Their names are put on a list of eligible candidates. An eligible's chances of getting a job depend on how high he stands on this list and how fast agencies are filling jobs from the list.

When a job is to be filled from a list of eligibles, the agency asks for the names of people on the list of eligibles for that job. When the civil service commission receives this request, it sends to the agency the names of the three people highest on this list. Or, if the job to be filled has specialized requirements, the office sends the agency the names of the top three persons who meet these requirements from the general list.

The appointing officer makes a choice from among the three people whose names were sent to him. If the selected person accepts the appointment, the names of the others are put back on the list to be considered for future openings.

That is the rule in hiring from all kinds of eligible lists, whether they are for typist, carpenter, chemist, or something else. For every vacancy, the appointing officer has his choice of any one of the top three eligibles on the list. This explains why the person whose name is on top of the list sometimes does not get an appointment when some of the persons lower on the list do. If the appointing officer chooses the second or third eligible, the No. 1 eligible does not get a job at once, but stays on the list until he is appointed or the list is terminated.

X. HOW TO PASS THE INTERVIEW TEST

The examination for which you applied requires an oral interview test. You have already taken the written test and you are now being called for the interview test – the final part of the formal examination.

You may think that it is not possible to prepare for an interview test and that there are no procedures to follow during an interview. Our purpose is to point out some things you can do in advance that will help you and some good rules to follow and pitfalls to avoid while you are being interviewed.

What is an interview supposed to test?

The written examination is designed to test the technical knowledge and competence of the candidate; the oral is designed to evaluate intangible qualities, not readily measured otherwise, and to establish a list showing the relative fitness of each candidate – as measured against his competitors – for the position sought. Scoring is not on the basis of "right" and "wrong," but on a sliding scale of values ranging from "not passable" to "outstanding." As a matter of fact, it is possible to achieve a relatively low score without a single "incorrect" answer because of evident weakness in the qualities being measured.

Occasionally, an examination may consist entirely of an oral test – either an individual or a group oral. In such cases, information is sought concerning the technical knowledges and abilities of the candidate, since there has been no written examination for this purpose. More commonly, however, an oral test is used to supplement a written examination.

Who conducts interviews?

The composition of oral boards varies among different jurisdictions. In nearly all, a representative of the personnel department serves as chairman. One of the members of the board may be a representative of the department in which the candidate would work. In some cases, "outside experts" are used, and, frequently, a businessman or some other representative of the general public is asked to serve. Labor and management or other special groups may be represented. The aim is to secure the services of experts in the appropriate field.

However the board is composed, it is a good idea (and not at all improper or unethical) to ascertain in advance of the interview who the members are and what groups they represent. When you are introduced to them, you will have some idea of their backgrounds and interests, and at least you will not stutter and stammer over their names.

What should be done before the interview?

While knowledge about the board members is useful and takes some of the surprise element out of the interview, there is other preparation which is more substantive. It *is* possible to prepare for an oral interview – in several ways:

1) Keep a copy of your application and review it carefully before the interview

This may be the only document before the oral board, and the starting point of the interview. Know what education and experience you have listed there, and the sequence and dates of all of it. Sometimes the board will ask you to review the highlights of your experience for them; you should not have to hem and haw doing it.

2) Study the class specification and the examination announcement

Usually, the oral board has one or both of these to guide them. The qualities, characteristics or knowledges required by the position sought are stated in these documents. They offer valuable clues as to the nature of the oral interview. For example, if the job involves supervisory responsibilities, the announcement will usually indicate that knowledge of modern supervisory methods and the qualifications of the candidate as a supervisor will be tested. If so, you can expect such questions, frequently in the form of a hypothetical situation which you are expected to solve. NEVER go into an oral without knowledge of the duties and responsibilities of the job you seek.

3) Think through each qualification required

Try to visualize the kind of questions you would ask if you were a board member. How well could you answer them? Try especially to appraise your own knowledge and background in each area, *measured against the job sought*, and identify any areas in which you are weak. Be critical and realistic – do not flatter yourself.

4) Do some general reading in areas in which you feel you may be weak

For example, if the job involves supervision and your past experience has NOT, some general reading in supervisory methods and practices, particularly in the field of human relations, might be useful. Do NOT study agency procedures or detailed manuals. The oral board will be testing your understanding and capacity, not your memory.

5) Get a good night's sleep and watch your general health and mental attitude

You will want a clear head at the interview. Take care of a cold or any other minor ailment, and of course, no hangovers.

What should be done on the day of the interview?

Now comes the day of the interview itself. Give yourself plenty of time to get there. Plan to arrive somewhat ahead of the scheduled time, particularly if your appointment is in the fore part of the day. If a previous candidate fails to appear, the board might be ready for you a bit early. By early afternoon an oral board is almost invariably behind schedule if there are many candidates, and you may have to wait. Take along a book or magazine to read, or your application to review, but leave any extraneous material in the waiting room when you go in for your interview. In any event, relax and compose yourself.

The matter of dress is important. The board is forming impressions about you – from your experience, your manners, your attitude, and your appearance. Give your personal appearance careful attention. Dress your best, but not your flashiest. Choose conservative, appropriate clothing, and be sure it is immaculate. This is a business interview, and your appearance should indicate that you regard it as such. Besides, being well groomed and properly dressed will help boost your confidence.

Sooner or later, someone will call your name and escort you into the interview room. *This is it.* From here on you are on your own. It is too late for any more preparation. But remember, you asked for this opportunity to prove your fitness, and you are here because your request was granted.

What happens when you go in?

The usual sequence of events will be as follows: The clerk (who is often the board stenographer) will introduce you to the chairman of the oral board, who will introduce you to the other members of the board. Acknowledge the introductions before you sit down. Do not be surprised if you find a microphone facing you or a stenotypist sitting by. Oral interviews are usually recorded in the event of an appeal or other review.

Usually the chairman of the board will open the interview by reviewing the highlights of your education and work experience from your application – primarily for the benefit of the other members of the board, as well as to get the material into the record. Do not interrupt or comment unless there is an error or significant misinterpretation; if that is the case, do not hesitate. But do not quibble about insignificant matters. Also, he will usually ask you some question about your education, experience or your present job – partly to get you to start talking and to establish the interviewing "rapport." He may start the actual questioning, or turn it over to one of the other members. Frequently, each member undertakes the questioning on a particular area, one in which he is perhaps most competent, so you can expect each member to participate in the examination. Because time is limited, you may also expect some rather abrupt switches in the direction the questioning takes, so do not be upset by it. Normally, a board member will not pursue a single line of questioning unless he discovers a particular strength or weakness.

After each member has participated, the chairman will usually ask whether any member has any further questions, then will ask you if you have anything you wish to add. Unless you are expecting this question, it may floor you. Worse, it may start you off on an extended, extemporaneous speech. The board is not usually seeking more information. The question is principally to offer you a last opportunity to present further qualifications or to indicate that you have nothing to add. So, if you feel that a significant qualification or characteristic has been overlooked, it is proper to point it out in a sentence or so. Do not compliment the board on the thoroughness of their examination – they have been sketchy, and you know it. If you wish, merely say, "No thank you, I have nothing further to add." This is a point where you can "talk yourself out" of a good impression or fail to present an important bit of information. Remember, *you close the interview yourself.*

The chairman will then say, "That is all, Mr. _____, thank you." Do not be startled; the interview is over, and quicker than you think. Thank him, gather your belongings and take your leave. Save your sigh of relief for the other side of the door.

How to put your best foot forward

Throughout this entire process, you may feel that the board individually and collectively is trying to pierce your defenses, seek out your hidden weaknesses and embarrass and confuse you. Actually, this is not true. They are obliged to make an appraisal of your qualifications for the job you are seeking, and they want to see you in your best light. Remember, they must interview all candidates and a non-cooperative candidate may become a failure in spite of their best efforts to bring out his qualifications. Here are 15 suggestions that will help you:

1) Be natural – Keep your attitude confident, not cocky

If you are not confident that you can do the job, do not expect the board to be. Do not apologize for your weaknesses, try to bring out your strong points. The board is interested in a positive, not negative, presentation. Cockiness will antagonize any board member and make him wonder if you are covering up a weakness by a false show of strength.

2) Get comfortable, but don't lounge or sprawl

Sit erectly but not stiffly. A careless posture may lead the board to conclude that you are careless in other things, or at least that you are not impressed by the importance of the occasion. Either conclusion is natural, even if incorrect. Do not fuss with your clothing, a pencil or an ashtray. Your hands may occasionally be useful to emphasize a point; do not let them become a point of distraction.

3) Do not wisecrack or make small talk

This is a serious situation, and your attitude should show that you consider it as such. Further, the time of the board is limited – they do not want to waste it, and neither should you.

4) Do not exaggerate your experience or abilities

In the first place, from information in the application or other interviews and sources, the board may know more about you than you think. Secondly, you probably will not get away with it. An experienced board is rather adept at spotting such a situation, so do not take the chance.

5) If you know a board member, do not make a point of it, yet do not hide it

Certainly you are not fooling him, and probably not the other members of the board. Do not try to take advantage of your acquaintanceship – it will probably do you little good.

6) Do not dominate the interview

Let the board do that. They will give you the clues – do not assume that you have to do all the talking. Realize that the board has a number of questions to ask you, and do not try to take up all the interview time by showing off your extensive knowledge of the answer to the first one.

7) Be attentive

You only have 20 minutes or so, and you should keep your attention at its sharpest throughout. When a member is addressing a problem or question to you, give him your undivided attention. Address your reply principally to him, but do not exclude the other board members.

8) Do not interrupt

A board member may be stating a problem for you to analyze. He will ask you a question when the time comes. Let him state the problem, and wait for the question.

9) Make sure you understand the question

Do not try to answer until you are sure what the question is. If it is not clear, restate it in your own words or ask the board member to clarify it for you. However, do not haggle about minor elements.

10) Reply promptly but not hastily

A common entry on oral board rating sheets is "candidate responded readily," or "candidate hesitated in replies." Respond as promptly and quickly as you can, but do not jump to a hasty, ill-considered answer.

11) Do not be peremptory in your answers

A brief answer is proper – but do not fire your answer back. That is a losing game from your point of view. The board member can probably ask questions much faster than you can answer them.

12) Do not try to create the answer you think the board member wants

He is interested in what kind of mind you have and how it works – not in playing games. Furthermore, he can usually spot this practice and will actually grade you down on it.

13) Do not switch sides in your reply merely to agree with a board member

Frequently, a member will take a contrary position merely to draw you out and to see if you are willing and able to defend your point of view. Do not start a debate, yet do not surrender a good position. If a position is worth taking, it is worth defending.

14) Do not be afraid to admit an error in judgment if you are shown to be wrong

The board knows that you are forced to reply without any opportunity for careful consideration. Your answer may be demonstrably wrong. If so, admit it and get on with the interview.

15) Do not dwell at length on your present job

The opening question may relate to your present assignment. Answer the question but do not go into an extended discussion. You are being examined for a *new* job, not your present one. As a matter of fact, try to phrase ALL your answers in terms of the job for which you are being examined.

Basis of Rating

Probably you will forget most of these "do's" and "don'ts" when you walk into the oral interview room. Even remembering them all will not ensure you a passing grade. Perhaps you did not have the qualifications in the first place. But remembering them will help you to put your best foot forward, without treading on the toes of the board members.

Rumor and popular opinion to the contrary notwithstanding, an oral board wants you to make the best appearance possible. They know you are under pressure – but they also want to see how you respond to it as a guide to what your reaction would be under the pressures of the job you seek. They will be influenced by the degree of poise you display, the personal traits you show and the manner in which you respond.

ABOUT THIS BOOK

This book contains tests divided into Examination Sections. Go through each test, answering every question in the margin. We have also attached a sample answer sheet at the back of the book that can be removed and used. At the end of each test look at the answer key and check your answers. On the ones you got wrong, look at the right answer choice and learn. Do not fill in the answers first. Do not memorize the questions and answers, but understand the answer and principles involved. On your test, the questions will likely be different from the samples. Questions are changed and new ones added. If you understand these past questions you should have success with any changes that arise. Tests may consist of several types of questions. We have additional books on each subject should more study be advisable or necessary for you. Finally, the more you study, the better prepared you will be. This book is intended to be the last thing you study before you walk into the examination room. Prior study of relevant texts is also recommended. NLC publishes some of these in our Fundamental Series. Knowledge and good sense are important factors in passing your exam. Good luck also helps. So now study this Passbook, absorb the material contained within and take that knowledge into the examination. Then do your best to pass that exam.

EXAMINATION SECTION

EXAMINATION SECTION
TEST 1

DIRECTIONS: Each question or incomplete statement is followed by several suggested answers or completions. Select the one that BEST answers the question or completes the statement. *PRINT THE LETTER OF THE CORRECT ANSWER IN THE SPACE AT THE RIGHT.*

Questions 1-5.

DIRECTIONS: Questions 1 through 5 are to be answered on the basis of the BUS RADIO TRANSMISSION CODE shown below.

BUS RADIO TRANSMISSION CODE

Buses are equipped with a 2-way radio system to aid the Bus Operator in the performance of his job. It is used primarily to transmit information to the Radio Dispatcher located in the Central Radio Operations Center. To assist the Bus Operator in the transmission of information without loss of time or possible confusion, the following Code is used:

Code Red Tag: To be used only in extreme emergency such as police assistance in the event of a hold-up, assault, serious vandalism, etc. The Bus Operator transmitting a Red Tag alert shall have priority over all other incoming calls. All other Bus Operators shall stand by until Dispatcher gives order to resume normal operations.
Code 1: Collision involving a bus.
Code 2: Passenger injured on board a bus.
Code 3: Disabled bus.
Code 4: Bus blocked by fire apparatus, other vehicle, parade, etc.

1. If a Bus Operator observes a mugging take place on his bus, he should radio a Code
   A. 1   B. 2   C. 4   D. Red Tag

2. If a passenger trips and hurts himself on a bus, the Bus Operator should radio a Code
   A. 1   B. 2   C. 3   D. Red Tag

3. If a bus is blocked by a street demonstration of marching adults, the Bus Operator should radio a Code
   A. 1   B. 2   C. 4   D. Red Tag

4. While a Bus Operator is reporting an injury to a passenger who fell and hurt his leg on the bus, a second Bus Operator interrupts this radio conversation with a Code Red Tag. The FIRST Bus Operator should
   A. continue with his message so that the passenger may be aided quickly
   B. repeat his message since the interruption may have scrambled his voice
   C. immediately stop talking
   D. ask the second Bus Operator to wait until he has completed his message

5. If a bus engine stalls and cannot be restarted, the Bus Operator should radio a Code

   A. 1 B. 2 C. 3 D. Red Tag

6. When a passenger deposits his fare into the fare box, the coins drop onto a tray. When this tray is tilted by the Bus Operator, it causes coins to drop into a cash box located beneath the tray. Bus Operators are required to tilt the tray after each fare is deposited so that the tray will be empty when the next passenger deposits his fare.
   The MOST logical reason for tilting the tray after each fare is to

   A. show the passengers that the money they deposit is being collected
   B. enable Bus Operators to see that each passenger deposits the correct fare
   C. prevent passengers from seeing how much money is in the fare box
   D. keep the tilt tray moving all the time so that it doesn't stick

7. An angry passenger getting off a bus at the front door loudly scolds the Bus Operator for not stopping at the preceding bus stop.
   If the Operator knows that the stop signal was not given until the bus was actually passing the preceding bus stop, the BEST action for him to take is to

   A. tell the passenger to wake up and give the stop signal in time
   B. tell the passenger to be quiet and not make a nuisance of himself
   C. call on the rest of the passengers to verify that the complaining passenger did not ring the stop signal in time
   D. avoid getting into an argument with this passe

8. A Bus Operator who is waiting on a two-way street to make a left-hand turn onto another street should

   A. turn his front wheels about 45 and keep his foot on the gas pedal
   B. turn his front wheels about 45 and keep his foot on the brake
   C. leave his front wheels facing straight ahead and keep his foot on the gas pedal
   D. leave his front wheels facing straight ahead and keep his foot on the brake

9. A Bus Operator notices that a child who is with her mother is playing with the exit signal bell cord. In this case, it would be BEST for the Bus Operator to

   A. ask the mother to stop her child from playing with the bell cord
   B. disconnect the bell cord until the mother and child get off the bus
   C. stop only at those bus stops where people are waiting or when he sees seated passengers on his bus stand up
   D. continue to stop at all bus stops in case someone actually wants to get off the bus

10. A passenger boards a bus and asks a seated passenger to remove his package from a seat so that he may sit down because there are no other empty seats. The seated passenger refuses the request and both passengers start arguing, which creates such a disturbance that the other passengers start complaining.
    In this situation, the Bus Operator should

    A. stop the bus until the problem is settled
    B. tell the seated passenger to remove his package
    C. order the seated passenger to pay another fare for the second seat
    D. tell the standing passenger to wait until another seat is available

11. A woman passenger is not paying attention and suddenly realizes that she has passed her stop. She asks the Bus Operator to let her off immediately.
    The Bus Operator would be using good judgment if he

    A. immediately stops the bus to let the woman off and makes no comment
    B. immediately stops the bus to let the woman off and warns her to be careful
    C. keeps driving and tells her he is only allowed to let her off at the next scheduled stop
    D. keeps driving and says nothing to her

12. While looking into the rear view mirror, a Bus Operator sees a man entering the bus from the rear door in order to avoid paying the required bus fare. The Bus Operator tells the man that he must pay the required fare or get off the bus.
    If the man agrees to pay the fare, it would be BEST for the Operator to

    A. order the man to get off the bus as a penalty for being dishonest
    B. insist that the man pay a double fare for causing a delay
    C. allow the man to ride free but warn him not to try to sneak on again
    D. collect the fare and continue along the bus route as scheduled

13. During rush hours, a Bus Operator is proceeding along his bus route with a full bus load of seated and standing passengers when someone rings the bell to get off. As he approaches the next bus stop, he sees a crowd of people waiting to get on the bus.
    In this situation, it would be BEST for the Operator to

    A. skip the stop and go directly to the next stop since there is no room for anyone else to enter the bus
    B. pull into the stop so that anyone wishing to get off the bus may do so
    C. go past the bus stop but stop the bus in the middle of the block so that passengers can get off the bus but no one else can get on
    D. pull into the stop and order the people closest to the door to take a transfer ticket and get off the bus to make more standing room

14. While driving on his route through a narrow street, a Bus Operator is forced to stop his bus because a large moving van is blocking the way. The driver of the van is jockeying the van back and forth in order to back it into a street-level loading platform. The stopping of the bus has caused cars to accumulate behind it, and the drivers of these cars start to blow their horns.
    In this case, the Bus Operator should

    A. signal the cars behind to back out of the street
    B. blow his horn also to hurry the van driver
    C. try to find a policeman so he can clear the street
    D. wait until there is sufficient clearance to drive past the van

15. On legal holidays when all public schools, banks, many private businesses, and federal, state, and city offices are closed, the Authority operates a reduced schedule. This means that buses arrive at bus stops less often because there are fewer buses running.
    Of the following, the MOST logical reason for having fewer buses running on legal holidays is that

    A. buses will not be in the way if there are parades on major streets
    B. there are usually fewer passengers riding the buses on legal holidays

C. more Authority employees will have the day off on legal holidays
D. the public will show respect for the legal holiday being observed

Questions 16-18.

DIRECTIONS: Questions 16 through 18 are to be answered on the basis of the explanation on HOW TO FIND THE STREET NEAREST A HOUSE NUMBER ON ANY AVENUE given below.

HOW TO FIND THE STREET NEAREST A HOUSE NUMBER ON ANY AVENUE

Take the house address number, drop the last figure, divide by 2, and add or subtract the key number given in the chart below.

For example: Near what cross street is 500 Fifth Avenue? Drop the last 0, divide the 50 by 2, and you get 25. Add the key number 18, and the result is 43. Therefore, Number 500 Fifth Avenue is nearest to 43rd Street.

Avenue	Key Number
First Ave.	Add 3
Fifth Ave.	Add 18
Sixth Ave.	Subtract 12

Avenue	Key Number
Amsterdam Ave.	Add 600
Lenox Ave.	Add 110
Madison Ave.	Add 26

16. Number 80 Amsterdam Ave. is NEAREST to _____ St.
 A. 20th B. 56th C. 64th D. 100th

17. Number 260 Sixth Ave. is NEAREST to _____ St.
 A. 1st B. 13th C. 16th D. 25th

18. Number 1064 Madison Ave. is NEAREST to _____ St.
 A. 41st B. 56th C. 63rd D. 79th

19. Bus Operators are not required to wear the official cap during the summer. The badge, which is ordinarily worn on the cap, must then be displayed on the right shoulder. The MOST likely reason for requiring the wearing of the badge on the right shoulder is that this location

 A. interferes least with the operation of the bus
 B. prevents the badge from being stolen
 C. reassures the passengers that the Operator is a good driver
 D. permits easy identification of the Operator

20. During snowstorms, Bus Operators are required to request passengers leaving the bus to *Please Be Careful and Watch Your Step.*
 The MOST likely reason for making this request is to

 A. avoid lawsuits in case of an accident
 B. alert passengers to the danger of slipping

C. warn the passengers that the rear door is for exit
D. improve relations with the public

21. Just after the Bus Operator of a Number 10 bus closes his doors at a bus stop, a man hammers with his fist on the front door demanding to get on the bus. After the Bus Operator opens the door, the man gets on and asks if the bus is a Number 15.
The Bus Operator would be practicing good public relations if he told the man

   A. to get off and check the number on the front of the bus
   B. that it is not a Number 15 bus and let the man off the bus
   C. that he cannot answer questions while the bus is in motion
   D. that he cannot answer now since the bus is behind schedule

21._____

22. A drunk boards a bus and refuses to pay his fare. While the Bus Operator is attempting to get the drunk to pay his fare, another passenger deposits the fare for the drunk saying that he is in a hurry.
The Bus Operator should

   A. refuse the fare since it was not paid by the proper person
   B. proceed on the way in a normal manner
   C. proceed until he comes upon a policeman and have him arrest the drunk
   D. put the drunk off the bus since he was causing a disturbance

22._____

23. A Bus Operator has requested the passengers to *Move to the Tear, please,* but the passengers continue to obstruct the entrance door even though there is considerable room in the rear of the bus.
The BEST course of action for the Bus Operator would be to

   A. stop the bus and tell all the passengers to get off the bus
   B. alternately brake and accelerate the bus to shake the passengers to the rear
   C. skip all stops until the passengers move
   D. continue to request that the passengers move to the rear so that others can get on

23._____

24. One of the Authority rules regarding lost property is that certain types of property should be held for not more than 8 hours and then must be sold or destroyed.
Of the following, the lost property that should come under this rule is a

   A. package of fresh fish   B. B. bottle of whisky
   C. suit of clothes   D. a can of peaches

24._____

Questions 25-30.

DIRECTIONS: Questions 25 through 30 are to be answered on the basis of the following schedules for Running Time and Headway. Running time is the scheduled time for a bus to travel from one stop to the next. For example, the running time between Twelfth Ave. and Fifteenth Ave. is 7 minutes when traveling Northbound and 8 minutes when traveling Southbound during the hours from 11:00 P.M. to 6:00 A.M.

Headway is the scheduled time between one bus and the next bus, which varies according to the time of day. For example, at Midnight the time between buses is 18 minutes. In answering these questions, refer to these schedules and assume that each bus proceeds on schedule.

Bus Stop	RUNNING TIME			
	11:00 P.M. to 6:00 A.M.		6:00 A.M to 11:00 P.M.	
	North-bound (going)	South-bound (returning)	North-bound (going)	South-bound (returning)
First Ave.	8	9	12	14
Fourth Ave.	5	6	9	10
Seventh Ave.	9	9	13	13
Ninth Ave.	5	6	9	10
Twelfth Ave.	7	8	11	12
Fifteenth Ave.				

HEADWAY		
From	To	Minutes
6:00 A.M.	9:30 A.M.	5
9:30 A.M.	4:30 P.M.	12
4:30 P.M.	6:00 P.M.	4
6:00 P.M.	11:00 P.M.	15
11:00 P.M.	6:00 P.M.	18

25. The bus leaving Fourth Ave., Northbound, at 11:30 A.M. is scheduled to arrive at Ninth Ave. at _____ A.M.

    A. 11:44   B. 11:45   C. 11:51   D. 11:52

26. The bus leaving Fifteenth Ave., Southbound, at 4:28 A.M. is scheduled to arrive at First Ave. at _____ A.M.

    A. 5:02   B. 5:06   C. 5:22   D. 5:27

27. If a passenger starting at First Ave. wanted to be at Twelfth Ave. by 12 Noon, he should board a bus that leaves no later than _____ A.M.

    A. 11:17   B. 11:19   C. 11:22   D. 11:23

28. At 10:00 P.M., a man who wants to board a bus at the corner of Fourth Ave. sees the bus pull away from the curb.
    For the NEXT bus, he should have a wait of _____ minutes.

    A. 5   B. 12   C. 15   D. 18

29. A bus which is on schedule becomes disabled at the Seventh Ave. bus stop at 11:45 M. The NEXT scheduled bus should arrive at this stop at

    A. 11:49 A.M.   B. 11:50 A.M.
    C. 11:57 A.M.   D. 12 Noon

30. A passenger who takes a bus at 8:30 A.M. usually arrives at work six or seven minutes late. He is supposed to be at work at 9:00 A.M.
    In order NOT to be late, he should take a bus which leaves his stop _____ minutes earlier.

    A. 5   B. 7   C. 10   D. 12

KEY (CORRECT ANSWERS)

1.	D	16.	C
2.	B	17.	A
3.	C	18.	D
4.	C	19.	D
5.	C	20.	B
6.	B	21.	B
7.	D	22.	B
8.	D	23.	D
9.	A	24.	A
10.	B	25.	D
11.	C	26.	B
12.	D	27.	A
13.	B	28.	C
14.	D	29.	C
15.	B	30.	C

TEST 2

DIRECTIONS: Each question or incomplete statement is followed by several suggested answers or completions. Select the one that BEST answers the question or completes the statement. *PRINT THE LETTER OF THE CORRECT ANSWER IN THE SPACE AT THE RIGHT.*

Questions 1-5.

DIRECTIONS: Questions 1 through 5 are to be answered on the basis of the following bulletin on SCHOOL ELIGIBILITY CARDS. In answering these questions, refer to this bulletin.

SCHOOL ELIGIBILITY CARDS

All Bus Operators are responsible for the proper use of School Eligibility Cards for reduced fares on their buses. These cards are issued to elementary and high school students. Such cards are good for the entire year from September 13 to June 28 next and are issued subject to the following conditions:

1. The card is to be used by the student whose name appears on the face of the card, and only on days when school is in session. If offered by any other person, it will be taken away by the Bus Operator and full fare will be collected from the person presenting the card.

2. The card will allow the student to ride on the particular bus indicated on the face of the card for a fare of fifty cents between 6 A.M. and 7 P.M. The fare of fifty cents must be deposited in the fare box by the student after the card is shown to the Bus Operator.

3. The student, after paying the fifty-cent fare, is entitled to the same transfer privileges as other passengers.

4. The card will be taken away if altered or misused, and the student will not be given a new card for a period of five school months.

5. The card is not good unless all entries on the card are made by the teacher and the card is signed by the teacher.

1. If a student's School Eligibility Card is taken away by a Bus Operator because of misuse, the student will
    A. never be issued a new card because of this misuse
    B. not be issued a new card until he pays for the old one
    C. be eligible for a new card after five school months
    D. be eligible for a new card if he gets a note from his teacher

2. A Bus Operator should take away a School Eligibility Card if it is presented
    A. at 9 A.M. before school opens
    B. at 3 P.M. after school opens
    C. by a college student
    D. more than twice a day

3. A Bus Operator should permit a student to ride at reduced fare if he presents his School Eligibility Card at

   A. 8:00 A.M. on Sunday
   B. 8:00 A.M. on Monday
   C. 8:00 P.M. on Saturday
   D. 8:00 P.M. on Wednesday

4. If a student presents a School Eligibility Card, pays a fifty-cent fare, and asks for a transfer, the Bus Operator should

   A. tell the student that during school hours he may not get a transfer
   B. tell him to use his School Eligibility Card instead
   C. give him a transfer if other passengers can get them free
   D. tell him he must pay the full $1.00 fare to get one

5. According to the above bulletin, School Eligibility Cards are NOT good on

   A. September 15
   B. October 26
   C. February 23 next
   D. June 30 next

Questions 6-15.

DIRECTIONS: Questions 6 through 15 are to be answered on the basis of the BUS OPERATOR'S DAILY TRIP SHEET shown below, which was turned in by a Bus Operator after the completion of his trip. At the control points shown, the Bus Operator made entries on this TRIP SHEET after taking readings of the cash counter and the token counter, which are part of his fare box. These counters show the total number of tokens collected and the total value of the coins placed in the fare box. Between the control points, the Bus Operator also noted the number of transfers he had collected and the number of children using students' bus passes since the last control point. Assume that all passengers were picked up at bus stops between control points and that students using bus passes were not required to pay an additional fare. Assume a fare of $1.00 and no charge for transfers.

BUS OPERATOR'S DAILY TRIP SHEET

Control Point	Leaves At	Cash	Difference	Tokens	Difference	Transfers Collected	Students' Bus Passes
Filmore Ave.	10:08 AM	0		0			
			$ 9.00		2	1	0
Flatlands Ave.	10:23 AM	$ 9.00		2			
			24.00		3	4	2
Kings Highway	10:59 AM	33.00		5			
			17.00		5	0	5
Glenwood Road	11:39 AM	50.00		10			
			12.00		0	2	1
Foster Ave.	12:19 PM	62.00		10			
			19.00		4	3	4
Church Ave.	12:55 PM	91.00		14			
			14.00		1	1	2
Linden Blvd.	1:10 PM	95.00		15			

6. The scheduled travel time between leaving Filmore Ave. and leaving Flatlands Ave. is _____ minutes.   6.____

   A. 10 B. 15 C. 36 D. 40

7. The scheduled travel time between leaving Foster Ave. and leaving Linden Blvd. is _____ minutes.   7.____

   A. 36 B. 41 C. 46 D. 51

8. The amount of cash collected between Filmore Ave. and Linden Blvd. was   8.____

   A. $14.00 B. $81.00 C. $95.00 D. $110.00

9. The total number of passengers carried between Filmore Ave. and Flatlands Ave. was   9.____

   A. 9 B. 10 C. 11 D. 12

10. The total number of tokens collected between Filmore Ave. and Church Ave. was   10.____

    A. 2 B. 5 C. 10 D. 14

11. The total number of persons paying a cash fare between Church Ave. and Linden Blvd. was   11.____

    A. 14 B. 15 C. 30 D. 95

12. The total number of school children who rode the bus by presenting a students' bus pass between Flatlands Ave. and Linden Blvd. was   12.____

    A. 12 B. 13 C. 14 D. 15

13. The total number of passengers carried on the trip from Filmore Ave. to Linden Blvd. was   13.____

    A. 76 B. 85 C. 105 D. 135

14. The GREATEST number of passengers paying a cash fare boarded the bus between   14.____

    A. Flatlands Ave. and Kings Highway
    B. Kings Highway and Glenwood Road
    C. Glenwood Road and Foster Ave.
    D. Foster Ave. and Church Ave.

15. The GREATEST number of persons got on the bus by use of transfers and students' bus passes and not by payment of a cash fare or tokens between   15.____

    A. Kings Highway and Glenwood Road
    B. Glenwood Road and Foster Ave.
    C. Foster Ave. and Church Ave.
    D. Church Ave. and Linden Blvd.

16. After a Bus Operator opens the doors at a bus stop, the first person on line stands in the doorway and asks for directions. After he receives the directions, the man asks for further details, and the people on the line start to complain about the delay.   16.____
    Of the following, it would be BEST for the Bus Operator to

    A. ask the people in the line to be quiet so that the man can be heard
    B. tell the man to wait for the next bus which will not be as crowded

C. refuse to give him the information until he pays his fare
D. give the man the details he requests

17. The rules of the Authority allow Bus Operators to wear glasses with tinted lenses except before sun-up and after sun-down.
The MOST likely reason for not allowing Bus Operators to wear tinted glasses before sun-up is that

   A. the Bus Operator may temporarily be blinded when the sun is coming up
   B. the use of tinted glasses at this time is poor public relations
   C. tinted lenses restrict the Bus Operator's vision at that time
   D. the passengers may think the Bus Operator has bad vision

18. While a bus is stopped for a traffic light at a busy intersection which is not a bus stop, a passenger pulls the stop cord several times and demands to be let off so he can catch a connecting bus that is passing by.
The BEST course of action for the Bus Operator would be to

   A. open the door and let the passenger out
   B. signal the connecting bus to wait for the passenger
   C. ignore the passenger
   D. tell the passenger that Bus Operators are allowed to open the doors only at bus stops

19. Bus Operators are forbidden to operate a bus while their right hand rests on the fare box.
The MOST likely reason for this rule is that resting a hand on the fare box

   A. is unsafe since both hands should be on the steering wheel
   B. prevents the deposit of fares in the fare box
   C. disturbs the passengers since the operator appears too relaxed
   D. may interfere with the forward view of the passengers

20. A rule of the Authority forbids Bus Operators from accepting fares by hand and requires that the Operator tell the passengers to put their fares in the fare box.
The MOST likely reason for this rule is to

   A. guarantee that all passengers deposit the correct fare
   B. reduce the chances of the fare being dropped onto the floor
   C. make sure that all fares are registered by the fare box
   D. prevent physical contact between the Bus Operator and the passengers

21. Passengers are allowed to play radios on Authority buses if the playing of the radio does not disturb other passengers.
If a young man is playing a radio very loudly and getting into arguments with other passengers who are complaining about the noise, the Bus Operator would be using good judgment if he

   A. tells the young man to turn the radio off completely and that he will be thrown off the bus if he turns it on again
   B. takes the radio away from the young man and tells him he can pick it up at the Authority headquarters

C. tells the young man to lower the volume of the radio
D. asks the passengers what radio station they would like to listen to and tells the young man to tune the radio to that station

22. A passenger boarding a bus has one foot on the bus and one foot still on the sidewalk. He is causing a delay of the bus while he is talking to someone who is not getting on the bus. This has been going on for some time, and the other passengers start complaining about the delay.
Of the following, it would be BEST for the Bus Operator to

   A. take his foot off the brake pedal and gently ease the bus forward, thereby informing the boarding passenger that he is causing a delay
   B. ignore the passengers who are complaining and allow the boarding passenger to finish his conversation
   C. close the doors halfway and then reopen them in order to force the boarding passenger to either get on or off the bus
   D. tell the boarding passenger that he should step aside and wait for the next bus if he wants to continue his conversation

22.___

23. A rule of the Authority states that: *A Bus Operator shall study maps and literature concerning the area along his bus route and the streets and points of interest nearby.* Of the following, the BEST reason for this rule is that the Bus Operator will

   A. be better able to drive his bus in the area
   B. become more interested in his work
   C. be better able to give correct information to passengers asking questions
   D. know how to re-route his bus in case of a tie-up on his regular route

23.___

24. Bus Operators must carefully inspect their buses before driving them out of the garage. All safety features, including the brakes, must be checked to see that they are in good working order.
The MOST important reason for this regulation is to

   A. provide for the safety of passengers
   B. protect the Authority from paying damages in accident cases
   C. improve the driving abilities of Bus Operators
   D. give the bus repairman work to do

24.___

25. Occasional unpleasant incidents with passengers who are insulting may be annoying to the Bus Operator.
Keeping this in mind, a newly-appointed Bus Operator should

   A. be suspicious of all passengers
   B. not be friendly with passengers at any time
   C. discourage passengers from asking questions by giving nasty replies
   D. try to remember the considerate passengers instead of the few inconsiderate ones

25.___

KEY (CORRECT ANSWERS)

1.	C	11.	A
2.	C	12.	C
3.	B	13.	D
4.	C	14.	A
5.	D	15.	C
6.	B	16.	D
7.	D	17.	C
8.	C	18.	D
9.	D	19.	A
10.	D	20.	C

21. C
22. D
23. C
24. A
25. D

———

EXAMINATION SECTION
TEST 1

DIRECTIONS: Each question or incomplete statement is followed by several suggested answers or completions. Select the one that BEST answers the question or completes the statement. *PRINT THE LETTER OF THE CORRECT ANSWER IN THE SPACE AT THE RIGHT.*

QUESTIONS 1-5.

The map shown on the following page represents a portion of the City of New York. Use this map to answer question 1 to 5.

1. The Verrazano Bridge is located at number 1.____
   A. 1   B. 2   C. 6   D. 17

2. Yankee Stadium is located at number 2.____
   A. 7   B. 8   C. 11   D. 15

3. The Lincoln Tunnel is located at number 3.____
   A. 2   B. 3   C. 5   D. 9

4. Kennedy Airport is located at number 4.____
   A. 4   B. 12   C. 13   D. 16

5. Coney Island is located at number 5.____
   A. 8   B. 10   C. 11   D. 14

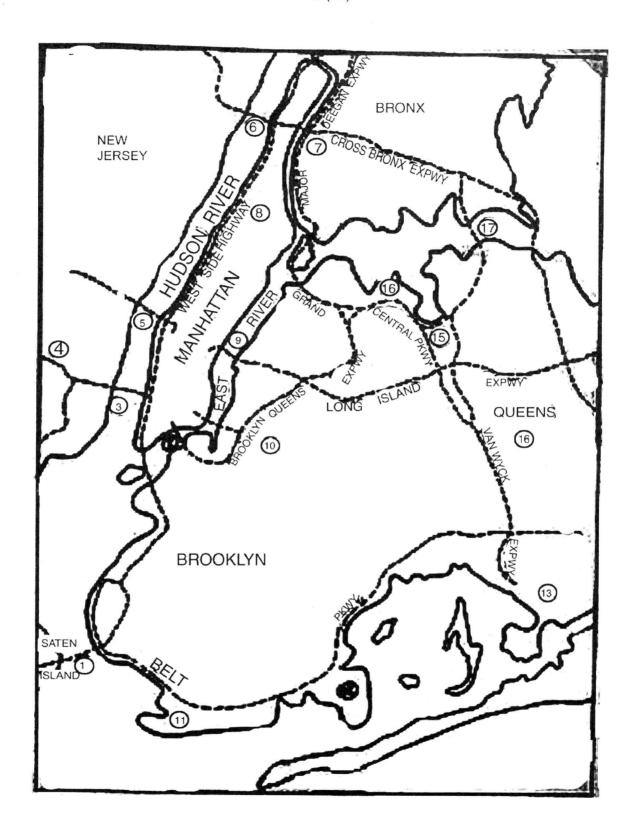

QUESTIONS 6-12.

Questions 6 to 12 deal with traffic situations which might be encountered by a Bus Operator. In each case, select the proper action to be taken. The meaning of each symbol used in the sketches is shown below. Note that the black dot (.) in a vehicle represents the driver of the vehicle. A vehicle not having a black dot indicates that there is no driver in the vehicle and that the vehicle is parked at the curb or double-parked.

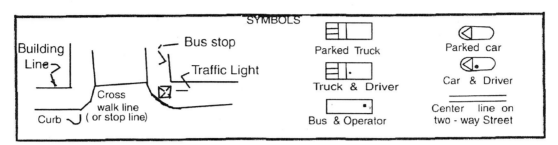

6. The vehicles on the north side of the street, including the bus, have stopped as shown because their traffic light has turned red. However, just after the Bus Operator stopped his bus, the fire alarm in the Fire House sounded, indicating that fire engines would start coming out of the Fire House. The action that the Bus Operator should IMMEDIATELY take is to

   A. pull in behind car No. 1
   B. move up alongside truck No. 2
   C. drive into the bus stop when truck No. 4 moves
   D. back up his bus under the guidance of a fireman

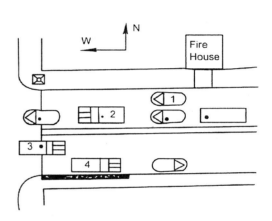

6.____

7. The sketch shows the condition of traffic with the buses stopped for a red light. If the indicator light on Bus No. 1 shows that it is going to make a left turn into B St., the Operator of Bus No. 2 should, when the light turns green

   A. sound his horn and continue along First Ave. since he has the right of way
   B. continue along his route *only* if he is behind schedule
   C. stay where he is until Bus No. 1 makes the turn since it has the right of way
   D. sound his horn and verbally warn the Operator of Bus No. 1 not to make the turn because he is in the wrong lane

7.____

8. If car No. 1 is pulling out of a parking space, the Bus Operator should

   A. sound his horn so that the car will not pull out into the traffic flow
   B. swing left over the center line to give the car ample room to pull out
   C. swing out sufficiently so as to be able to pass car No. 1
   D. slow up and let car No. 1 pull out

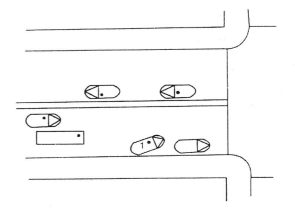

9. If the Bus Operator sees that there is a parked car in the bus stop, he should open his doors for the discharge of passengers

   A. where he is
   B. directly behind the parked car
   C. in front of the parked car
   D. alongside the parked car

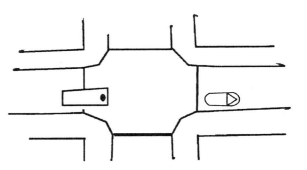

10. If the bus is ready to pull away from the bus stop, the Bus Operator should

    A. pull out quickly before car No. 4 blocks the way
    B. pull up behind car No. 2
    C. wait until car No. 4 passes before pulling out
    D. wait until car No. 2 moves on

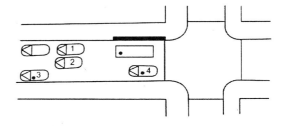

11. The sketch shows the condition of traffic just before the light turns green for the bus. There is traffic congestion ahead of car No. 2 which prevents it from moving. When the light turns green the Bus Operator should
    A. pull in behind car No. 1
    B. drive up beside car No. 4
    C. slowly creep up behind car No. 4
    D. remain where he is until car No. 4 moves up

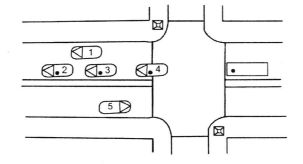

12. The bus shown in the sketch is traveling at twenty miles per hour along Main Street. If the traffic light for the bus turned from green to yellow when the bus reached the location shown, it would be BEST for the Bus Operator to

    A. stop where he is
    B. turn right into Ave. C
    C. wait until the cars on Ave. C pass, then proceed
    D. continue past the light, without stopping

12.____

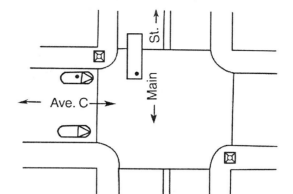

QUESTIONS 13-21.

Questions 13-21 refer to the Bus Map on the following page which shows the routes of various buses. The Bus Route Number is shown by a number within a box (R-2) and the route followed by the bus is shown as a box a broken line(■ ■ ■ ■) Use this map to answer questions 13 to 21.

13. If you are at the Tunnel located in the lower right part of the map and want to go MOST directly to the Skating Rink located in the upper left part of the map, you should take bus number

    A. R-12   B. R-14   C. R-16   D. R-18

13.____

14. If you are at Main St. and 29th St. and want to go MOST directly to the World Court at 18th St. and Ave. B you should take bus number

    A. R-5   B. R-7   C. R-9   D. R-11

14.____

15. If you are at the Bridge located on the upper right side of the map and want to go MOST directly to the Medical Center at 9th St. and Ave. B, you should take bus number

    A. R-2   B. R-4   C. R-6   D. R-8

15.____

16. If you are at the Tunnel located in the lower right part of the map and want to go MOST directly to the Museum at 44th St. and Ave. H, you should take bus number

    A. R-12   B. R-14   C. R-16   D. R-18

16.____

17. If you are at Main St. and 28th St. and want to go MOST directly to Union Station at 22nd St. and Ave. F, you should take bus number

    A. R-5   B. R-7   C. R-9   D. R-11

17.____

18. If you are at the Bridge located in the upper right side of the map and want to go MOST directly to the Sports garden at 10th St. and Ave. J, you should take bus number

    A. R-6   B. R-7   C. R-9   D. R-18

18.____

19. If you leave the Sports Garden at 10th St. and Ave. J and want to go MOST directly to 44th St. and Ave. B, you should take bus number 19.___

   A. R-7 and change to the R-10
   B. R-8 and change to the R-12
   C. R-9 and change to the R-14
   D. R-6 and change to the R-12

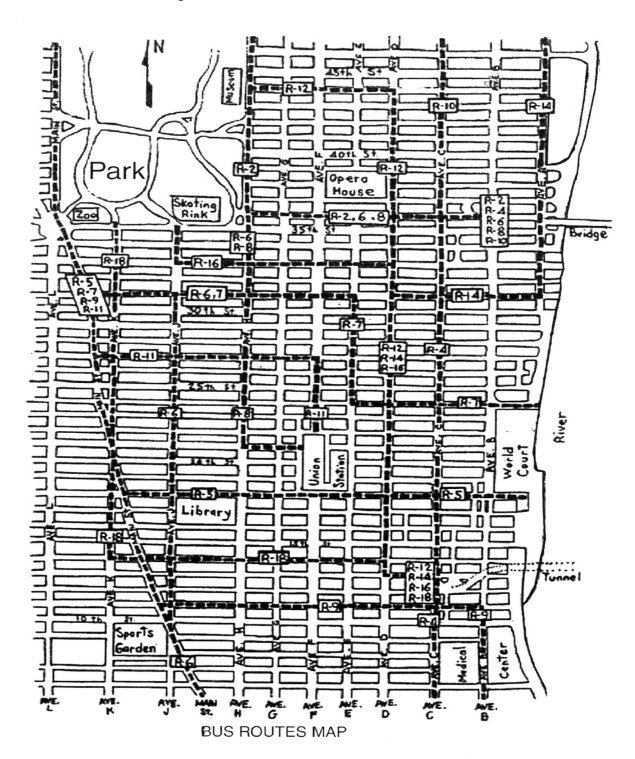

BUS ROUTES MAP

20. If you leave Union Station at Ave. F and 18th St. and want to go MOST directly to the Museum at 44th St. and Ave. H, you should take bus number

    A. R-11 and change to the R-8
    B. R-11 and change to the R-6
    C. R-5 and change to the R-2
    D. R-5 and change to the R-12

21. If you leave the Opera House at Ave. D and 37th St. and want to go MOST directly to the Zoo in the Park located in the upper left side of the map, you should take bus number

    A. R-12 and change to the R-16
    B. R-12 and change to the R-11
    C. R-6 and change to the R-16
    D. R-8 and change to the R-7

22. At the scene of a bus accident, a Bus Operator is questioned by a man claiming to be a newspaper reporter. The Bus Operator would be using good judgment if he

    A. cooperates fully with the reporter since this would show good will on the part of the transit authority
    B. first checks the reporter's credentials and then gives him any information which will eventually be included in a transit authority accident report
    C. gives the desired information *only* on the understanding that he will NOT be quoted
    D. refers the reporter to the proper officials of the transit authority

QUESTIONS 23-25.

Questions 23-25 deal with descriptions of various types of motor vehicle accidents. In each of these questions, select the sketch which most accurately represents the word description of the accident given in the question. The meaning of each symbol given in the sketches is shown below.

```
                              Symbols
Car:  ▷        Pedestrian:  ○      Path and Direction BEFORE accident   ──────▶
Bus:  ▷        Tree  ●             Path and Direction AFTER accident    ─ ─ ─▶
```

23. Car #2 and the bus were proceeding north on Ave. M, with Car #2 tailgating the bus. Car #1 was proceeding east on Peck St. When the bus stopped suddenly to avoid hitting Car #1, it was immediately struck from behind by Car #2. Car #1 continued east on Peck St. while both Car #2 and the bus stopped after the collision.

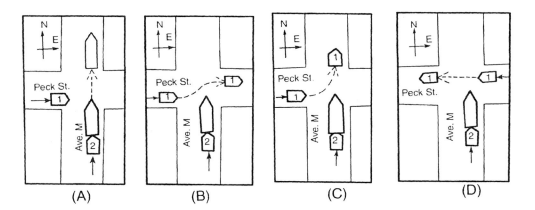

24. Mr. Jones was crossing Baker Street when he was struck by a bus approaching from his right. After hitting Mr. Jones, the bus swerved left and ran into a tree.

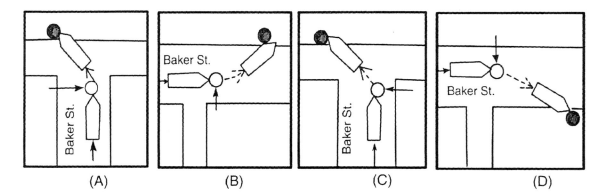

25. While a Bus Operator was driving his bus on a two-way street, a child suddenly ran out in front of the bus from between two parked cars. To avoid hitting the child, the Bus Operator swung his bus sharply to the left. By so doing, the bus crossed the center line and crashed head-on into an oncoming car. The collision caused the car to swing to the right and into the curb.

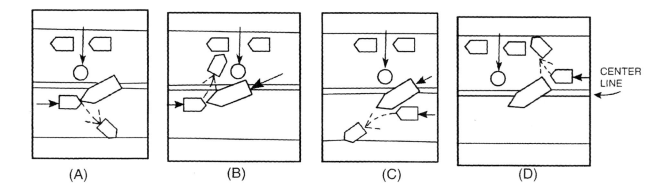

KEY (CORRECT ANSWERS)

1.	A	11.	D
2.	A	12.	D
3.	C	13.	C
4.	C	14.	A
5.	C	15.	B
6.	D	16.	A
7.	A	17.	D
8.	D	18.	A
9.	C	19.	D
10.	C	20.	D

21. D
22. D
23. B
24. A
25. A

EXAMINATION SECTION
TEST 1

DIRECTIONS: Each question or incomplete statement is followed by several suggested answers or completions. Select the one that BEST answers the question or completes the statement. *PRINT THE LETTER OF THE CORRECT ANSWER IN THE SPACE AT THE RIGHT.*

Questions 1-3.

DIRECTIONS: Questions 1 through 3 are to be answered on the basis of the following schedule for running time. Running Time is the scheduled time for a bus to travel from one stop to the next. The arrow indicates the direction in which the bus travels. For example, the running time from Main St. to School St., eastbound, is 5 minutes during the hours from 10:00 P.M. to 6:00 A.M., and 9 minutes from 6:00 A.M. to 10:00 P.M. If you want to know when a bus that leaves School St. at 11:00 P.M. should arrive at Pearl St., you should add the 14 minutes running time to 11:00 P.M. to obtain 11:14 P.M.

RUNNING TIME

Bus Stop	10:00 PM to 6:00 AM Eastbound	10:00 PM to 6:00 AM Westbound	6:00 AM to 10:00 PM Eastbound	6:00 AM to 10:00 PM Westbound
Main St. to School St.	5	6	9	11
to Bank St.	4	5	7	18
to Market St.	5	6	10	12
to Pearl St.	5	6	9	11
to State St.	4	5	7	8
Totals	23	28	42	50

1. An eastbound bus leaves School St. at 1:30 P.M. At what time will it arrive at Market St.? _____ P.M.

   A. 1:39   B. 1:41   C. 1:47   D. 1:50

2. If a passenger boarding a westbound bus at State St. wishes to be at Bank St. by 3:00 P.M., the last bus he should take is one that leaves no later than _____ P.M.

   A. 2:21   B. 2:29   C. 2:34   D. 2:43

3. A westbound bus leaves Pearl St. at 11 P.M. but has an 18 minute delay because of a sick passenger at Market St. The bus is delayed for another 4 minutes due to a broken traffic light at School St. What time will the bus arrive at Main St.?

   A. 11:45 P.M.   B. 11:50 P.M.
   C. 12:07 A.M.   D. 12:15 A.M.

4. To help prevent passenger accidents inside a bus, which of the following starting and stopping procedures should a bus operator follow?
   _____ acceleration when starting and _____ when stopping.

   A. Gradual; gradual slowing down
   B. Rapid; rapid braking
   C. Gradual; rapid braking
   D. Rapid; gradual slowing down

5. When a bus operator is driving a bus, a flashing yellow light at an intersection means that he should

   A. stop
   B. stop, then proceed slowly
   C. proceed with caution
   D. maintain his speed through the intersection

Questions 6-8.

DIRECTIONS: Questions 6 through 8 are to be answered on the basis of the following schedule for Headway. Headway is the scheduled time between one bus and the next bus, and this varies according to the time of day. For example, from 12 Noon to 4 P.M., the time between buses is 10 minutes, and from 5:00 A.M. to 9:00 A.M., it is 5 minutes.

HEADWAY

			Minutes
5:00 A.M	to	9:00 A.M	5
9:00 A.M	to	12:00 Noon	8
12:00 Noon	to	4:00 P.M	10
4:00 P.M	to	7:00 P.M	5
7:00 P.M	to	11:00 P.M	15
11:00 P.M	to	5:00 A.M	30

6. At 7:00 A.M., a man just misses a bus.
   About how many minutes will he have to wait for the next bus?

   A. 5   B. 8   C. 9   D. 11

7. At 8:33 P.M., a woman arrives at a bus stop. The last bus left her stop on schedule 3 minutes ago. The next scheduled bus has been cancelled due to faulty equipment. The bus following the cancelled bus is running three minutes late because of heavy traffic.
   At what time should another bus arrive at the woman's stop?

   A. 8:40 A.M.   B. 8:57 P.M.   C. 9:03 P.M.   D. 9:06 P.M.

8. What is the difference between the headway times at 11:50 A.M. and 11:20 P.M.?
   _____ minutes

   A. 15   B. 20   C. 22   D. 25

9. In heavy traffic, which of the following turn situations is potentially MOST hazardous? 9.____

   A. Right turn from one two-way street onto another two-way street
   B. Left turn from a one-way street onto a two-way street
   C. Right turn from a two-way street onto a one-way street
   D. Left turn from one two-way street onto another two-way street

10. As you approach an intersection in your bus, you note that the traffic light is red and you hear the wailing noise of an ambulance siren. A police officer at the intersection motions for you to go through the light. Under the circumstances, you should 10.____

    A. stop until you can determine the location of the ambulance
    B. stop until the light turns green, then proceed
    C. proceed to the middle of the intersection and stop so that you can better determine the location of the ambulance
    D. proceed through the intersection

11. Which of the following actions should a bus operator take if he notices a boy climbing on the back of his bus? 11.____

    A. Reduce speed and continue on his route
    B. Make sudden stops and starts to shake the boy off
    C. Stop the bus, inform his passengers why he is stopping, and then order the boy off the bus
    D. Ignore the boy and continue his trip at a normal speed

Questions 12-15.

DIRECTIONS: Questions 12 through 15 are to be answered on the basis of the following schedule. Running time is the scheduled time for a bus to travel from one stop to the next. The arrow indicates the direction in which the bus travels. For example, the running time from the Railroad Station to Main & Oak is 5 minutes. Lay-over time is the time spent at the terminal before leaving on the next trip.

Bus Stop	Southbound Running Time (Minutes)		Northbound Running Time (Minutes)	
Railroad Station	(leaves)		5	
Main & Oak	5		4	
Main & Elm	4		6	
Main & Ash	6		3	
Main & Pine	3		5	
Main & Birch	5		4	
Farmer's Market	4		8	
Plum & State	8		7	
Apple & State	7		7	
Pear & State	7		6	
Peach & State	6		5	
Court House	5		(leaves)	

Note: Layover time at each of the terminals, *Railroad Station Terminal* and *Court House Terminal*, is 5 minutes.

12. What is the running time, in minutes, from Peach & State northbound to Main & Ash? 12.___

   A. 37　　　B. 40　　　C. 42　　　D. 45

13. If a bus leaves the Railroad Station at 8:10 A.M., at what time should it arrive at the Court House? 13.___
   _____ A.M.

   A. 9:05　　　B. 9:08　　　C. 9:10　　　D. 9:12

14. If a bus leaves the Court House at 9:05 A.M., at what time should it arrive at Farmer's Market? 14.___
   _____ A.M.

   A. 9:30　　　B. 9:35　　　C. 9:38　　　D. 9:43

15. How much time will it take a bus leaving Main & Pine southbound to arrive back at Main & Pine on the return trip? 15.___
   1 hour, _____ minutes

   A. 17　　　B. 19　　　C. 29　　　D. 33

Questions 16-20.

DIRECTIONS: Questions 16 through 20 are to be answered SOLELY on the basis of the BUS OPERATOR'S DAILY TRIP SHEET shown below. At each terminal, at the end of a trip, the operator takes the readings on the cash counter and fare card counter which are part of the fare box and enters them on the BUS OPERATOR'S DAILY TRIP SHEET. The part of the BUS OPERATOR'S DAILY TRIP SHEET shown below is a record of the fare box readings for a specific working day for Bus Operator Birch. Note that a trip covers the distance from one terminal to the other. When Operator Birch left the Rowland Street terminal for the first trip of his working day, the cash counter registered $677.25 from a previous operator's run, and the fare card counter registered 113 fares. Birch left Rowland Terminal at 12:51 P.M. and completed his first trip over the route and arrived at the Tully Street Terminal at 1:28 P.M. Assume that at each terminal arriving and leaving times are identical. For the remainder of his working day, he rode back and forth along his route, arriving at the Rowland and Tully terminals at the times indicated on the BUS OPERATOR'S DAILY TRIP SHEET. His fare box readings were taken and entered on the trip sheet shown below immediately upon arrival at the terminals. When answering these questions, assume the fare is $2.25 and that all passengers are required to pay the full fare. Also assume that the card fares collected are worth $2.25 each.

BUS OPERATOR'S DAILY TRIP SHEET

POINT LEAVING FROM	TIME	FARE BOX READINGS AT THE END OF EACH TRIP	
		CASH	CARDS
Rowland Street Terminal	12:51 PM	677.25	113
Tully Street Terminal	1:28 PM	756.00	117
Rowland Street Terminal	2:08 PM	810.00	122
Tully Street Terminal	2:45 PM	893.25	131
Rowland Street Terminal	3:25 PM	987.75	133
Tully Street Terminal	4:04 PM	1,102.50	144
Rowland Street Terminal	4:38 PM	1,212.75	147
Tully Street Terminal	5:18 PM	1,233.00	148

16. How much cash was collected between 1:28 P.M. and 3:25 P.M.? 16.____

    A. $198.75   B. $228.75   C. $231.75   D. $326.25

17. How many fares were collected between 2:45 P.M. and 4:38 P.M.? 17.____

    A. 16   B. 17   C. 25   D. 147

18. What is the value of the card fares collected from 12:51 P.M. to 5:18 P.M.? 18.____

    A. $74.25   B. $78.75   C. $81.00   D. $83.25

19. How many passengers got on the bus between 2:08 P.M. and 4:04 P.M.? 19.____

    A. 144   B. 152   C. 157   D. 176

20. What was the total number of passengers carried during the entire run from 12:51 P.M. to 5:18 P.M.? 20.____

    A. 245   B. 269   C. 282   D. 583

Questions 21-27.

DIRECTIONS: Questions 21 through 27 are to be answered SOLELY on the basis of the description of the accident and the ACCIDENT REPORT shown below and on the following page. The ACCIDENT REPORT contains 38 numbered spaces. Read the description and look at the ACCIDENT REPORT before answering these questions.

Description of Accident: At 1:15 P.M., on July 20, 2011, an auto with license plate# 51VOMNY, driven by Martha Ryan, license number R21692-33739 295897-41, and owned by George Ryan, traveling east on Fulton Street, crashed into the right front wheel of a moving Flxible bus, T.A. Vehicle No. 7026, license plate no. 10346-K, at the inter-section of Jay Street and Fulton Street. The bus was covering Run 12 on Route B67. The auto was a green 2004 Chevrolet Malibu. The bus with 15 passengers was traveling south on Jay Street. The bus had a green traffic light in its favor at the Jay St. - Fulton St. intersection. The bus driver was Art Simmons, Badge No. 5712, license number S 24368 35274 263 745-42.

    Two passengers in the bus fell onto the floor. An elderly woman (age 65) bruised her left knee. A male (age 25) bruised the palm of his right hand. The auto driver's daughter, Mary (age 19), who was in the right front seat, bumped her head on the windshield. The police and an ambulance were summoned. The three injured persons were taken to Cumberland Hospital by Attendant John Hawkins. Police Officer Thomas Brown, Badge No. 2354, from the 68th Precinct, took statements from witnesses to the accident.

6 (#1)

ACCIDENT REPORT
TO BE FILLED IN BY BUS OPERATOR

Route _1_ Run _2_ T.A. Vehicle Type: Bus Truck Auto Other Vehicle _3_ T.A. Vehicle No. _4_ T.A. License Plate No. _5_ Make _6_ Date of Accident _7_ Hour _8_ Street Lights On _9_
Place of Accident _____10_____
Direction of T.A. Vehicle _11_ Direction of Other Vehicle _12_
State if operating on one- or two-way street: T.A. Vehicle _13_ way
                                    Other Vehicle _14_ way
Did accident occur in bus stop area? _____15_____
JNumoer 01 passengers in T.A. Vehicle _16_
JNumber of persons in other vehicle _17_
Trallic lights involved _18_ Color of same when leaving near corner _19_ Was ambulance called?
_20_ Persons taken to what hospital? ___21___
Was police officer present? _22_ Officer's No. _23_ Precinct _24_
Name of owner of other vehicle _25_
License No. of other vehicle _26_
Address of owner of other vehicle _____27_____
color ol other vehicle _28_ Model of other vehicle ___29___
Year of other vehicle _30_ Make of other vehicle ___31___
Name of driver of other vehicle _____32_____
Address of driver of other vehicle _____33_____
License JNo. of driver of other vehicle _____34_____
Uther driver male or female _____35_____
BUS OPERATOR IDENTIFYING INFORMATION: PASS # _36_; BADGE # _37_;
                                    LICENSE # _38_

21. Which of the following should be entered in Space 4?   21.____

    A. B67   B. 12   C. 7026   D. 10346K

22. Which of the following should be entered in Space 12?   22.____

    A. North   B. South   C. East   D. West

23. Which of the following should be entered in Space 16?   23.____

    A. 10   B. 12   C. 15   D. 67

24. Which of the following should be entered in Space 24?   24.____

    A. 62   B. 67   C. 68   D. 2354

25. Which of the following should be entered in Space 28?   25.____

    A. Red   B. Blue   C. Yellow   D. Green

26. Which of the following should be entered in Space 32?   26.____

    A. Martha Ryan   B. Mary Ryan
    C. George Ryan   D. John Hawkins

27. Which of the following should be entered in Space 37?   27.____

    A. 2354   B. 5712   C. 51 VOM-NY   D. 5127

28. An angry passenger scolds Bus Operator George Smith for not stopping at a bus stop. Smith did not hear the passenger signal, but there was a lot of traffic noise and he realizes the passenger might have signalled.
    Of the following, the BEST action for the bus operator to take is to

    A. keep driving, say nothing, and stop at the next bus stop for which he hears a signal
    B. stop the bus immediately and let the passenger off
    C. tell the passenger in no uncertain terms to signal clearly in the future and, as a lesson to the passenger, skip the next stop as well
    D. explain that he did not hear a signal and let the passenger off at the next stop

28.____

29. As a bus approaches a crowded bus stop, an elderly passenger sitting with a cane near the front of the bus rings the bell to get off.
    Which of the following is the BEST action for the bus operator to take?

    A. Stop short of the bus stop, let the elderly passenger out the front door, then pull into the bus stop.
    B. Pull into the bus stop, open the front and rear doors, and tell the elderly passenger to walk to the rear door to get off.
    C. Pull into the bus stop, open the doors, and tell the crowd, *Please let this passenger off.*
    D. Pull into the bus stop, let the crowd on first, then permit the elderly passenger to get out the front door.

29.____

30. At an intersection with no traffic control device, which of the following has the right-of-way over the others?
    A

    A. pedestrian in a crosswalk
    B. vehicle making a right turn
    C. vehicle approaching the intersection
    D. bus crossing the intersection

30.____

Questions 31-35.

DIRECTIONS: Questions 31 through 35 are to be answered SOLELY on the basis of the EXCLUSIVE LANE RULES printed below.

EXCLUSIVE LANE RULES

Bus Operators using the exclusive bus and taxi lane westbound to the Howard Tunnel in the eastbound roadway of the Porter Express-way should be guided by the following rules:

1. Headlights must be turned on just before entering the bus lane.
2. Speed must not exceed 35 miles per hour. Police will enforce this limit.
3. At least a 200-foot spacing must be maintained behind the vehicle ahead.
4. If a traffic cone is in the lane, drive over it. Do not attempt to go around it and do not stop your bus.
5. Lane hours are only from 7:00 A.M. to 10:00 A.M. Do not enter at any other time or if the lane is closed.
6. Do not leave the lane at any time, not even to pass a disabled vehicle, except under police direction.

7. Do not open doors or discharge passengers from a disabled bus until police assistance has arrived.
8. Any Transit Authority bus in the exclusive lane able to accommodate discharged passengers from a disabled bus of <u>any</u> company will do so without requiring payment of additional fare.

31. Transit Authority Bus Operator James Hanzelik is operating his bus in the exclusive bus and taxi lane. He is carrying 25 passengers and has room for about 40 more. Hanzelik comes upon an Antelope Bus Company bus which has broken down in front of him in his lane. The Antelope bus has 20 passengers in it. Hanzelik stops his bus. A short time later, a police officer arrives on the scene.
Bus Operator Hanzelik should pass the disabled bus under the direction of the police officer after first

    A. taking on the passengers from the disabled bus without charge
    B. taking on the passengers of the disabled bus and charging each of them the difference between the Transit Authority fare and the Antelope Bus Company fare
    C. politely declining to take on the passengers of the disabled bus because it is not a Transit Authority bus
    D. taking on the passengers of the disabled bus and charging each of them the regular Transit Authority fare

32. You are driving a bus in the exclusive bus and taxi lane. If you observe a traffic cone in the middle of your lane, you should

    A. stop your bus and place the traffic cone where it belongs
    B. go around the traffic cone to avoid destroying it
    C. drive over the traffic cone
    D. call for the police to move the traffic cone

33. Bus Operator Peter Globe is traveling in the exclusive bus and taxi lane when his bus becomes disabled. He stops his bus in the lane and phones for police assistance. While he is waiting for the police to arrive, another bus in the same lane pulls up behind him. The second bus has enough room to accommodate his passengers. After consulting with the other bus operator, he transfers his passengers to the second bus without charging an additional fare.
Bus Operator Globe's action was

    A. *proper;* because the other bus had sufficient room to accommodate his passengers
    B. *improper;* because he transferred the passengers without police assistance
    C. *proper;* because both buses stayed in the exclusive lane
    D. *improper;* because he did not charge his passengers an additional fare

34. A bus operator driving his bus legally in the exclusive bus and taxi lane should have his headlights on

    A. only when he is passing another vehicle
    B. only when the driver ahead is driving too slowly
    C. if his speed exceeds 35 miles per hour
    D. at all times

35. Bus Operator Hector Gonzalez is driving his bus in the exclusive bus lane when he has to stop because of a disabled auto blocking his way. The auto had been traveling eastbound in the next lane but got a flat tire and came to a stop in the exclusive lane. Gonzalez waits until the police arrive to guide him around the disabled auto. After the police guide Gonzalez around the disabled auto, they leave. In order to reach the Howard Tunnel before 10:00 A.M., Bus Operator Gonzalez drives at 40 miles an hour and keeps a distance of 250 feet behind a taxi. He arrives at the Howard Tunnel without incident. His action was

    A. *proper;* because the lane hours are from 7:00 A.M. to 10:00 A.M.
    B. *improper;* because his speed exceeded 35 miles per hour
    C. *proper;* because he made up for lost time in maintaining his schedule
    D. *improper;* because he should not have waited for the police to guide him

35.____

KEY (CORRECT ANSWERS)

1.	C	16.	C
2.	B	17.	A
3.	A	18.	B
4.	A	19.	B
5.	C	20.	C
6.	A	21.	C
7.	C	22.	C
8.	C	23.	C
9.	D	24.	C
10.	D	25.	D
11.	C	26.	A
12.	B	27.	B
13.	C	28.	D
14.	C	29.	C
15.	C	30.	A

31.	A
32.	C
33.	B
34.	D
35.	B

TEST 2

DIRECTIONS: Each question or incomplete statement is followed by several suggested answers or completions. Select the one that BEST answers the question or completes the statement. *PRINT THE LETTER OF THE CORRECT ANSWER IN THE SPACE AT THE RIGHT.*

Questions 1-2.

DIRECTIONS: Questions 1 and 2 are to be answered SOLELY on the basis of the information contained in the following two rules.

1. Bus operators must be relieved only at designated relief points and at the time specified in schedules, unless otherwise instructed by the proper authority. They must never leave their bus until properly relieved, and must not, under any circumstance, surrender the bus to another employee apparently unfit for duty.

2. If a passenger becomes disorderly, annoying, or dangerous, this passenger must be asked to leave the bus at the next designated bus stop.

1. Bus Operator Herbert Bacon is worried about his teenaged daughter who underwent a serious operation. He wants to phone his wife at the hospital to find out how his daughter is feeling. At a designated bus stop, he parks the bus and goes into a tobacco store to use the public telephone.
His action was

   A. *proper;* because he parked in a designated bus stop
   B. *improper;* because he left the bus with no bus operator in charge
   C. *proper;* because the nature of the situation justified the phone call
   D. *improper;* because he could have used a telephone in the street

2. Bus Operator Wendy Green notices that a passenger who is obviously drunk is annoying the other passengers with his loud and embarrassing remarks. She asks him several times to be quiet, but he continues to bother the passengers.
Bus Operator Green should stop the bus _____ and ask the drunken passenger to get off.

   A. immediately
   B. at the next dispatcher's station
   C. at the next red light
   D. at the next designated bus stop

3. Oak Street is one-way northbound and is intersected by Elm Street, which is one-way eastbound.
If there are no traffic control devices at the intersection, and if traffic allows, it should be permissible to make a

   A. right turn from Elm Street into Oak Street
   B. right turn from Oak Street into Elm Street
   C. left turn from Oak Street into Elm Street
   D. four corner U-turn at the intersection

Questions 4-11.

DIRECTIONS: Questions 4 through 11 are to be answered by consulting the Bus Map on the following page. Notice that the left edge of the map is divided into spaces with letters, and the bottom edge of the map is divided into spaces with numbers. The lines for a space with a letter and the lines for a space with a number if extended across the map would meet and form a quadrant (or area). As an example, look at the sketch below which represents part of the map and note that the quadrant formed by an extension of the lines which are the boundaries of the F space and of the 2 space meet to form the F2 quadrant. In this quadrant on your map, you can find Lutheran Medical Center. The locations referred to in the questions below can be found within the quadrants shown in parentheses.

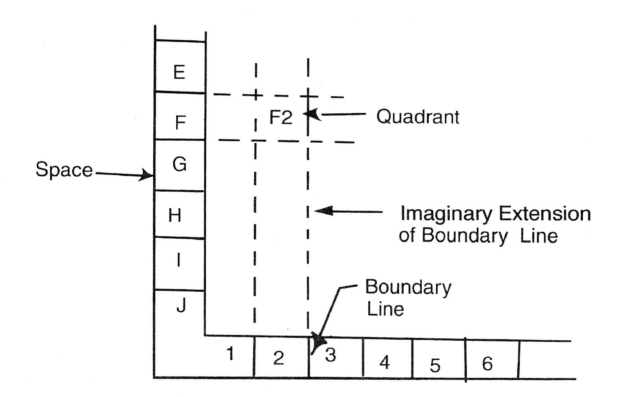

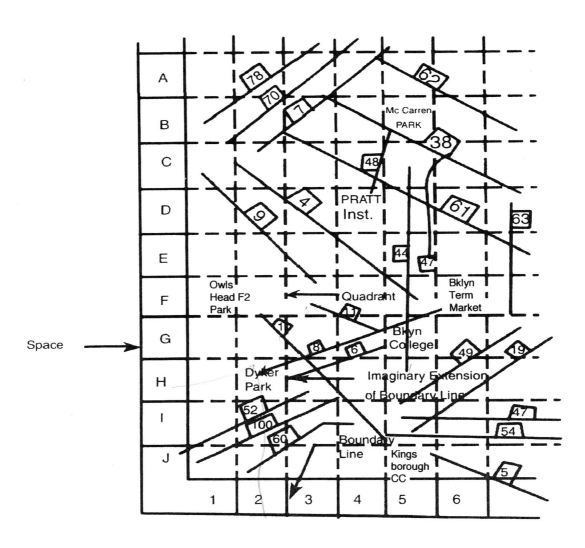

4. Which bus route goes from Brooklyn Terminal Market (quadrant F6) to Dyker Beach Park (quadrant H2)?

   A. 78   B. 8   C. 70   D. 7

5. Which bus route goes from Pratt Institute (quadrant D4) to McCarren Park (quadrant B5)?

   A. 62   B. 38   C. 48   D. 61

6. Which bus should you take to go from Kingsborough Community College (quadrant J5) to Owls Head Park (quadrants F1 and F2)?

   A. 1   B. 4   C. 9   D. 49

7. Which bus route goes from Brooklyn College (quadrant G5) to the intersection of 49th Street and 8th Avenue (quadrant F3)?

   A. 6   B. 11   C. 44   D. 70

8. Which bus route goes from the intersection of 79th Street and Kings Highway (quadrant H3) to Brooklyn College (quadrant G5)?

   A. 6   B. 14   C. 38   D. 52

9. Which bus route goes from the intersection of Flushing Avenue and Nostrand Avenue (quadrant C5) to the inter-section of Nostrand Avenue and Quentin Road (quadrant H5)?

   A. 100   B. 62   C. 48   D. 44

10. Which bus route goes from the intersection of Empire Blvd. and Rogers Avenue (quadrant E5) to the intersection of Myrtle Avenue and Throop Avenue (quadrant C5)?

    A. 44   B. 47   C. 49   D. 54

11. Which bus route goes from the intersection of Ovington Avenue and Fifth Avenue (quadrant G2) to the intersection of 86th Street and Bay Parkway (quadrant H3)?

    A. 1   B. 6   C. 5   D. 63

Questions 12-14.

DIRECTIONS: Questions 12 through 14 are to be answered SOLELY on the basis of the following SCHOOL BUS BULLETIN.

SCHOOL BUS BULLETIN

Anywhere in the state, including the city, when the red lights of a school bus flash, you must stop your vehicle before reaching the bus. This is the law, whether you are approaching the bus from the front, or overtaking it from the rear. In fact, you must stop even if the school bus is on the far side of a four-lane divided highway. Children might cross the road after getting off or before getting on the school bus, and they don't always stop to check in both directions before crossing. They depend on you, the motorist, to stop as the law requires. If the red lights of a school bus are flashing, you may pass it only if the school bus driver clearly signals you to do so, or you are directed to do so by a police officer.

12. It is evening rush hour during a very hot day. The bus you are operating is 15 minutes behind schedule because of very heavy traffic. The air conditioning system in your bus has broken down, and your passengers are uncomfortable, annoyed, and anxious to get home. You are on a wide, two-way street, and you approach a school bus which is parked with its red lights flashing on the other side of the street. The school bus driver is at the wheel, but you see no children in the bus or anywhere on the street.
    Under the circumstances, you should _____ the school bus.

    A. proceed with caution past
    B. proceed with normal speed past
    C. stop your bus before reaching
    D. radio for a police officer to direct you past

13. You are a bus operator on a two-lane, one-way main street. You are in the left lane stopped in back of an automobile at a red light. In the lane to your right and in front of you is a school bus which is also waiting for the red light to change. There is no police officer at the corner. When the light changes to green, the car in front of you moves through the

intersection, but the school bus stalls and will not start. It does not flash its red lights. Under the circumstances, you may

- A. pass the school bus because its red lights are not flashing
- B. not pass the school bus because there may be children in it
- C. pass the school bus only if the school bus driver signals for you to do so
- D. not pass the school bus because there is no police officer on the scene

14. You are operating a Transit Authority bus on a one-way street. You approach a school bus from the rear. It is parked at the right curb with its red lights flashing. The school bus is almost filled with children, although a few more are waiting on the sidewalk to get on. After you stop your bus, the school bus driver, who is seated at the wheel of his bus, signals you to pass on the left. Under the circumstances, it would be

- A. *proper* for you to pass the school bus because its driver signalled for you to do so
- B. *improper* for you to pass the school bus because children were still boarding
- C. *proper* for you to pass the school bus because most of the children were already inside the bus
- D. *improper* for you to pass the school bus because its red lights were flashing

Questions 15-17.

DIRECTIONS: Questions 15 through 17 are to be answered SOLELY on the basis of the BULLETIN shown below.

COLORS OF MONTHLY ELEMENTARY AND REDUCED FARE SCHOOL TICKETS - SUMMER 2011

For the summer of 2011, the colors of the tickets for the School Fare Program for school children will be as follows:

Monthly Elementary School Tickets
Elementary pass FREE - no payment of fare required.
July   - Blue with Blue Date
August   - Rose with Blue Date

High School Eligibility Cards
Students will pay 50 cents going to school in the A.M. and 50 cents on the return trip from school in the P.M. the entire Summer Session.
July   - Beige (Green *S*)
August   - Yellow (Green *S*)

Type #2 (r) & #3 (c) Rapid Transit Surface Extension
High school students presenting reduced fare passes for all Rapid Transit Surface Extension Routes - B/42, B/54, B/35, BX/55, and Q/49, will be required to pay $1 in the A.M. on the way to school for the entire Summer Session, July 6, 2011 through August 14, 2011.

15. Joe is a second year high school student attending the Summer Session. If he boards a bus on Wednesday, July 23, he

- A. can ride free if he has a valid Blue ticket with Blue Date
- B. must pay 50 cents and show a Beige (Green *S*) card

C. must pay 50 cents and show a Blue (Green S) card
D. must pay 50 cents and show a Yellow (Green S) card

16. Mary is a senior in high school attending the Summer Session. 16._____
When she boards the Surface Extension Route B/54 on her way to taking the train to school, she must show her reduced fare pass and pay

   A. no fare   B. 50¢   C. $1   D. $7.50

17. George, a junior in high school, and his brother, Tyrone, in 5th grade, are both attending 17._____
the Summer Session.
If they board a bus on Tuesday, August 4th, the bus operator should look for a _____ ticket and a _____ card.

   A. rose; yellow   B. blue; beige
   C. blue; blue   D. rose; beige

18. You are a bus operator driving your bus at normal route speed. Suddenly, a man in a 18._____
sportscar cuts sharply in front of you and continues to speed away from you.
Which of the following actions would it be BEST for you to take now?

   A. Accelerate to catch up to the sportscar, then cut it off.
   B. Get the license number of the sportscar and radio a report to the police.
   C. Slow down until the sportscar is at least a quarter mile ahead of you.
   D. Continue along your route at normal speed.

Questions 19-21.

DIRECTIONS: Questions 19 through 21 are to be answered SOLELY on the basis of the REVERSE BUS MOVEMENT PROCEDURE shown below.

REVERSE BUS MOVEMENT PROCEDURE

Bus Operators may operate a bus in reverse only if they determine that no other turn or movement is possible. When operating in reverse, Bus Operators must follow all of the following steps in this procedure.

   1. The movement in reverse must not be made until the bus operator has walked around to the back of the bus and made a visual inspection of the area behind the bus.
   2. The bus operator must be guided by a responsible person, such as a police officer or another bus driver.
   3. The person guiding the bus operator must station himself near the left rear of the bus.
   4. When the bus operator has determined that it is safe to back up, he will signal by giving three toots of the horn immediately before starting the reverse movement.

19. Bus Operator Charles Waters has stopped directly behind a disabled bus and cannot 19._____
move around the bus without backing up. Waters remains in his seat and asks a police officer to stand at the left rear of the bus to direct him. Waters toots his horn three times and slowly backs up just enough to go around the disabled bus.
Bus Operator Water's actions in backing up the bus were IMPROPER because Waters

   A. was not guided back by a responsible person
   B. should have gotten permission from a supervisor before backing up

C. tooted his horn just before backing up
D. did not inspect the area behind the bus before backing up

20. Bus Operator Elaine Strollin determines that it is necessary to operate her bus in reverse. She inspects the area to the rear of her bus and determines that it is safe to back up. She toots her horn three times to attract the attention of a police officer to assist her in backing up the bus. The police officer goes to the proper position to direct Operator Strollin. With the passengers still in her bus, Operator Strollin is directed by the police officer and backs up her bus without incident .
Operator Strollin's actions in backing up the bus were

   A. *proper* because she had followed the complete procedure for a reverse bus movement
   B. *improper* because she did not discharge her passengers before backing up
   C. *proper* because with a police officer present, the complete procedure for a reverse bus movement need not be followed
   D. *improper* because she did not toot her horn three times just before backing up

21. A bus operator has decided that he must back up his bus. The operator has asked a responsible person to guide his bus back.
Where should he ask that person to stand?

   A. In front of the bus
   B. On the right side of the bus near the front door
   C. At the left rear of the bus
   D. At the right rear of the bus

22. A careful driver should allow 20 feet of stopping room for each ten miles an hour of speed. When driving at night, you should be able to stop within the roadway distance illuminated by your headlights.
If your headlights illuminate the roadway approximately 90 feet before you, your speed at night should NOT exceed about _____ miles per hour.

   A. 25   B. 35   C. 45   D. 55

Questions 23-24.

DIRECTIONS: Questions 23 and 24 are to be answered on the basis of the following bulletin.

The Culture Bus Loops operate on Saturdays, Sundays, and some holidays. The buses on Culture Bus Loop I (M41) run on the loop through midtown and uptown Manhattan every 30 minutes during the winter and every 20 minutes during the summer, from 10:00 A.M. to 6:00 P.M., and make 22 stops. You may get off at any one of the stops, take in the sights, and then catch a later bus, or you can simply stay on the bus for the entire loop. Culture Bus Loop II (B88) provides another view of New York City, one that includes midtown and lower Manhattan, and some of Brooklyn as well. The buses on this loop run every 30 minutes, from 9:00 A.M. to 6:00 P.M. Running time is approximately 2 hours and 25 minutes. Tickets for the Culture Buses may be bought only on the buses. Since the driver cannot make change, and since our fare boxes will not accept paper currency, please have your $2.50 fare in any combination of silver or tokens and silver. The Culture Bus Loop I ticket is valid for certain transfer privileges to crosstown buses. By using the crosstown buses, you may tailor your day's itinerary. The Culture Bus Loop I ticket is also valid as an extension to and from the Cloisters on the M4 bus from Stop 10.

23. The Culture Loop II bus (B88) goes into which borough or boroughs? 23.____

    A. Brooklyn and Manhattan
    B. Brooklyn and Queens
    C. Manhattan *only*
    D. Manhattan and the Bronx

24. The Culture Bus Loop I ticket is also valid on the M4 bus as an extension to and from 24.____

    A. Brooklyn Heights
    B. the Cloisters
    C. Greenwich Village
    D. Staten Island

25. A bus that is traveling at 22 MPH with 30 passengers has a green light as it approaches an intersection. Just as the bus enters the intersection, the light changes from green to yellow. 25.____
    Which of the following is the BEST action for the bus operator to take?

    A. Stop short, back his bus out of the intersection, wait for the light to turn green again, then drive through the intersection.
    B. Stop quickly, wait in the intersection for the light to turn green again, then drive through the inter-section .
    C. Continue through the intersection at 22 MPH.
    D. Speed up to get through the intersection before the light turns red.

26. You are driving your bus down a one-way street during the rush hour, and you are already 5 minutes behind schedule. You find that you must stop your bus because the street is blocked by a parcel delivery truck which is double-parked, and the driver is not in sight. 26.____
    Which of the following is the FIRST action you should take?

    A. Try to attract the attention of the truck driver by blowing your horn.
    B. Back the bus out of the street.
    C. Radio the police for a tow truck to come and haul away the parcel delivery truck.
    D. Jump out of the bus and knock on the door of the house nearest to the parked truck.

27. A bus operator is behind schedule. He has closed his doors and is about to pull out of a bus stop and cross an intersection. The green light is about to change. 27.____
    An elderly man raps on the door of the bus. The operator realizes that if he opens the door for the man to board, he will miss the light and get even further behind schedule.
    Which of the following is the BEST action for the bus operator to take?

    A. Pull away from the bus stop and continue on his route.
    B. Go through the intersection before the light changes, then wait for the elderly man to cross the street and board his bus.
    C. Open the door and let the man board the bus.
    D. Open the door, let the man onto the bus, and tell the man he should have waited for the next bus.

Questions 28-29.

DIRECTIONS: Questions 28 and 29 are to be answered SOLELY on the basis of the information contained in the bulletin shown below on AIR POLLUTION.

AIR POLLUTION

No bus operator should permit the gasoline or diesel engine of his bus to discharge air-polluting gases while the bus is stationary at a route terminal. Operators must shut off bus engines, unless otherwise directed, immediately upon completing arrival at the terminal stop. All operators and supervisors should remain constantly alert for any Transit Authority vehicles emitting excessive fumes while in motion. They should report such vehicles immediately on their bus radios to Surface Control by bus number, together with any further available identifying information.

28. Nathan Pearl, a bus operator, is driving his bus along Flatbush Avenue when he notices black smoke being discharged from the exhaust of a bus coming in the opposite direction.
    Of the following, what should Bus Operator Pearl do?

    A. Let the bus operator of the other bus take care of it.
    B. Tell the other operator about the pollution when he sees him in the garage after they have completed their runs.
    C. Call Surface Control to report the bus which is emitting black smoke.
    D. Write a report on the bus emitting black smoke when he completes his run, giving the bus number and other identifying information.

29. To avoid air pollution, bus operators are ordered to do which of the following?

    A. Drive no more than 12 miles an hour.
    B. Shut off the engine at bus stops where a large number of passengers are boarding and alighting.
    C. Shut off the engine at terminal stops.
    D. Close all windows of the bus so that passengers will not breathe in smoke or fumes being emitted by the bus.

30. A bus operator notices a wallet on the floor next to the driver's seat. While waiting at the next red light, he examines the contents of the wallet. It has $30 worth of bills and various cards identifying the owner as Charles Bergen.
    Of the following, it would be MOST appropriate for the bus operator to

    A. hold onto the wallet during the run and return it if a passenger tells him he has lost his wallet and identifies himself as Charles Bergen
    B. ask passengers if anyone has lost a wallet, and then return the wallet if a person who identifies himself as Charles Bergen claims to have lost the wallet and can identify its contents
    C. pocket the money and inconspicuously place the wallet back on the floor. Anyone careless enough to drop his wallet deserves no sympathy.
    D. ask if anyone on the bus has lost a wallet with $30 in cash and return it if someone claims to have lost it

31. You are a bus operator. While you are stopped at a red light, a woman on board your bus, speaking English with a heavy foreign accent, asks you for directions. You do not understand her question.
    Of the following, you should

    A. ask the woman to repeat her question more slowly
    B. ask one of the other passengers to give directions to the woman

- C. hand the woman a bus map of the borough you are in
- D. give the woman the phone number of the Transit Authority Travel Information Bureau

32. As you are driving your bus, you notice that traffic is close behind you. On a sidewalk about 150 feet ahead of you, some children are playing with a small rubber ball. Suddenly, the ball rolls into the street in the path of your bus.
Which of the following actions should you take?

- A. Brake lightly, honk your horn, and be prepared to stop short if a child races after the ball.
- B. Honk your horn and stop short in anticipation that one of the children might run after the ball.
- C. Honk your horn and continue at normal speed, but be prepared to brake quickly.
- D. Honk your horn, then speed up so as to get past the children as quickly as possible.

33. Your bus is 15 minutes behind schedule. The bus scheduled to follow yours has gotten ahead of you and is in the next bus stop. You wish to pass this bus. As you approach the bus stop, you notice that this bus is starting to pull out.
You should

- A. honk your horn and pass the bus quickly
- B. pull behind the bus and allow it to continue ahead
- C. pull alongside the bus and tell the driver that you would appreciate it if he did not pass you again
- D. make a turn to a lightly traveled parallel street going in your direction, then drive non-stop for several blocks to both pass the bus in front of you and get back on schedule

34. You are carrying 20 passengers in your bus on a one-way two-lane street. You notice that the car ahead of you is weaving erratically in and out of its lane.
Of the following, your MOST appropriate course of action is to

- A. keep a big enough distance between the car and your bus to eliminate any possibility of contact
- B. stay close behind the car and keep honking your horn until the driver of the car either pulls over to a curb or turns down a side street
- C. stay as close behind the car as you can and be prepared to signal the first police officer you see
- D. pass the car and speed away from it

35. Your bus is approaching an intersection with the green light in your favor. From the street on your right, a man on a bicycle is approaching the intersection. The man has sufficient time to stop at the intersection.
Of the following, the BEST action for you to take is to

- A. exercise your right of way and cross the intersection at normal speed
- B. stop and wait until you see what the cyclist does
- C. proceed with caution, ready to apply brakes if necessary
- D. accelerate through the light before the cyclist reaches the intersection

KEY (CORRECT ANSWERS)

1.	B	16.	C
2.	D	17.	A
3.	B	18.	D
4.	B	19.	D
5.	C	20.	D
6.	A	21.	C
7.	B	22.	C
8.	A	23.	A
9.	D	24.	B
10.	B	25.	C
11.	A	26.	A/C
12.	C	27.	C
13.	A	28.	C
14.	A	29.	C
15.	B	30.	B

31.	A
32.	A
33.	B
34.	A
35.	C

EXAMINATION SECTION
TEST 1

DIRECTIONS: Each question or incomplete statement is followed by several suggested answers or completions. Select the one that BEST answers the question or completes the statement. *PRINT THE LETTER OF THE CORRECT ANSWER IN THE SPACE AT THE RIGHT.*

1. A conductor's indication board indicates to the conductor of a MAXIMUM length train whether

    A. the motorman has stopped the train properly within the station platform limits
    B. the door trouble is electrical or mechanical
    C. any of his indication lights is malfunctioning
    D. his train is drummed properly

    1.____

2. A conductor who finds that a public address system microphone is defective should

    A. notify the dispatcher immediately
    B. notify the desk trainmaster immediately
    C. try to repair the damage
    D. report it on the terminal car defect sheet

    2.____

3. If a conductor operating a 10-car train with married pairs finds that he can no longer operate from the middle position, he must

    A. discharge the passengers
    B. operate from the 6th car
    C. operate from the 8th car
    D. call the tower

    3.____

4. A conductor who is assigned to platform duty finds it necessary to leave his assigned post in an emergency. He should report that he is leaving his post to the nearest train dispatcher or the

    A. station supervisor
    B. desk trainmaster
    C. crew dispatcher
    D. platform conductor

    4.____

5. When a conductor finds a firearm on a train or platform, the firearm must be

    A. personally delivered by the conductor to the lost property office
    B. sent to the most convenient location equipped with lost property bags
    C. turned over to the transit police
    D. forwarded by special messenger to the lost property office

    5.____

6. If a motorman overruns the station platform, causing a few doors to be past the station platform, he should

    A. back up the train using the conductor as a flagman
    B. assist the conductor with the exiting passengers
    C. call the station department for instructions
    D. call the terminal train dispatcher for instructions

    6.____

7. At a terminal, three amber (orange) lights are called _____ lights.

    A. indication   B. gap
    C. holding   D. starting

8. Four short blasts of a train horn means that the train

    A. is answering a signal
    B. crew needs assistance
    C. is passing caution lights
    D. is requesting a route or signal

9. An emergency telephone can be found by looking for a

    A. red light   B. blue light
    C. red and white sign   D. blue and white sign

10. If a train is approaching a river tube from which dense smoke is coming, the motorman should

    A. ask the desk trainmaster whether he should enter the tube
    B. discuss entering the tube with the conductor
    C. not enter the tube under any condition
    D. unload passengers immediately

11. In the event of a delay, the train crew must use the public address system, where provided, to inform the passengers.
The first announcement must occur within the first 10 minutes of the delay, and subsequent announcements must be made EVERY _____ minutes.

    A. 2   B. 5   C. 10   D. 15

12. When a 10-car train is leaving the station, the conductor should observe the station platform until the train has moved _____ car length(s).

    A. 1   B. 2   C. 3   D. 4

13. A succession of short blasts from a train horn could mean that the train

    A. is making an irregular movement through the station
    B. is answering a signal
    C. needs a road car inspector
    D. has vandals aboard

14. The train buzzer signal consisting of one long buzz

    A. means stop
    B. means proceed
    C. is an answer to any signal
    D. means that the train has vandals aboard

15. If a motorman loses indication after he has left the terminal, he should

    A. immediately take the train out of service
    B. travel at a reduced speed

C. keep the train in service only with the desk trainmaster's permission
D. keep the train in service if the conductor's indication is working

16. A no clearance area along the right of way is indicated by a sign that

    A. has blue and white diagonal stripes
    B. has blue and yellow diagonal stripes
    C. has red and white diagonal stripes
    D. is all red

17. A motorman is LEAST likely to take orders from a

    A. dispatcher
    B. station supervisor
    C. towerman
    D. conductor

18. A conductor operating a train during non-rush hours discovers that he has a hanging guard light.
    If he is unsuccessful when following the prescribed instructions for correcting the trouble, he should

    A. ask the passengers to leave the train
    B. notify the tower
    C. direct the passengers to the good section of the train, and the defective section should then be isolated
    D. stay in service only if he can get a road car inspector

19. Before a conductor leaves a train to go onto a station platform, he must FIRST

    A. notify the nearest dispatcher
    B. notify the desk trainmaster
    C. open a conductor's emergency valve
    D. open the train doors

20. The train buzzer signal consisting of two short buzzes

    A. means stop
    B. means proceed
    C. is an answer to any signal
    D. means that the motorman should signal for a road car inspector

21. If an end door is unlocked on an R-44 car, it is indicated by a lighted _____ light.

    A. red   B. blue   C. yellow   D. green

22. The train buzzer signal consisting of three short buzzes means that the

    A. motorman should signal for a policeman
    B. motorman should signal for a road car inspector
    C. train has run by the station platform
    D. motorman should signal for a signal maintainer

23. When an angry passenger asks for a conductor's badge number, the conductor should

    A. make a report to the proper authorities
    B. try to convince the passenger that he isn't at fault

C. try to get at the root of the problem
D. give his badge number without delay

24. When a conductor is assigned to a lay-up train, he has certain specified duties. The one that has the LOWEST priority is

    A. removing discarded newspapers
    B. closing all storm doors
    C. closing all windows
    D. closing all ventilators

25. If a certain conductor earns $540.00 a week and works 40 hours, his salary per hour is

    A. $15.00   B. $12.75   C. $13.50   D. $14.25

26. A revenue train is a train that is used for

    A. picking up money collected by railroad clerks
    B. carrying passengers
    C. collecting garbage
    D. transporting lost articles

27. If a leader is ahead of schedule during rush hour, it is MOST likely that the follower will

    A. have a lighter load of passengers than usual
    B. not be affected
    C. have a heavier load of passengers than usual
    D. also be ahead of schedule

28. When a motorman on a local train fails to stop at a local station, the conductor should IMMEDIATELY

    A. buzz the motorman
    B. apply the hand brakes
    C. open a conductor's emergency valve
    D. notify the passengers

29. Of the following, the one that is NOT a required condition when trains are running on flooded tracks is that the

    A. desk trainmaster must give permission
    B. trains must run with extreme caution
    C. water must be below the ball of the running rail
    D. conductor must flag at the head of the train

30. When a train makes a stop at a station, the conductor MUST keep his doors open for at least _____ seconds.

    A. 3   B. 5   C. 8   D. 10

31. A train is scheduled to leave the terminal at a certain time. The conductor must be at his operating position before this time by AT LEAST _____ minutes.

    A. 2   B. 4   C. 6   D. 10

32. The remote control for the main car lights of a train operates from 32._____

    A. 600 volts DC   B. 120 volts AC
    C. a 32-volt battery   D. a 600-volt battery

33. If a passenger is observed on the tracks without permission, the FIRST thing a conductor should do is 33._____

    A. call the police department   B. use the emergency alarm box
    C. use the emergency telephone   D. sound the train horn

34. When power has been removed from a section of track, the only one authorized to restore it is the 34._____

    A. desk trainmaster   B. man who removed the power
    C. power department supervisor   D. safety officer

35. In the course of performing his duties, a conductor should have the LEAST need for 35._____

    A. train schedules   B. general orders
    C. train register sheets   D. work programs

36. When one contact shoe of a train car is touching the contact rail, the number of live shoes on that car is 36._____

    A. 1   B. 2   C. 4   D. 8

37. In a ten-car train equipped with drum switches, the number of drum switches that must be in the OFF position when the train is in service is 37._____

    A. 1   B. 2   C. 10   D. 20

38. In a ten-car train equipped with drum switches, the number of drum switches that should be in the THRU position when the train is in service is 38._____

    A. 2   B. 10   C. 16   D. 20

39. A train buzzer signal will sound at locations where the drum switch is in the _____ position. 39._____

    A. Full   B. Thru
    C. Off   D. Release

40. Which of the following is not permitted on subway platforms and stairwells? 40._____

    A. Talking on a cell phone
    B. Touching subway signage
    C. Assisting other riders with directions
    D. Smoking cigarettes

41. When the motorman's indication is lit, it means that 41._____

    A. all side doors are closed and locked
    B. the conductor is getting indication
    C. the train brake has been released
    D. there is trouble in at least one of the train cars

42. The color of the motorman's indication is

    A. red   B. green   C. white   D. yellow

43. The color of the conductor's indication is

    A. red   B. green   C. white   D. yellow

44. When an exterior guard light on a train car is lit, it DEFINITELY means that

    A. all doors are closed and properly locked
    B. at least one door is not closed or properly locked
    C. a door is being held open by a passenger
    D. the doors on one side of the train car are closed and properly locked

45. When an interior guard light in a train car is lit, it DEFINITELY means that

    A. all doors are closed and properly locked
    B. at least one door is not closed or properly locked
    C. a door is being held open by a passenger
    D. the doors on one side of the train car are closed and properly locked

46. When a flagman moves a yellow flag up and down, it means that the motorman should

    A. stop
    B. call the tower
    C. proceed very slowly
    D. back up

47. The color of the caution lights that a flagman places on the side of the track is

    A. red   B. green   C. white   D. yellow

48. Conductors who are on duty are permitted to wear tinted glasses

    A. in the tunnels after a physician has examined them
    B. in the open, during daylight hours only
    C. only if they also carry a pair of untinted glasses
    D. at no time

49. Passengers must be removed from a train when the brakes are cut out on more than _____ of its cars.

    A. 1   B. 1/5   C. 1/3   D. 1/4

50. The definition of *headway* is the

    A. length of station stop time of a train
    B. running time of a train
    C. difference between the scheduled and actual time of a run
    D. scheduled time interval between trains

KEY (CORRECT ANSWERS)

1. A	11. B	21. B	31. A	41. A
2. D	12. C	22. B	32. C	42. C
3. A	13. A	23. D	33. B	43. A
4. B	14. A	24. A	34. A	44. B
5. C	15. D	25. C	35. C	45. B
6. B	16. C	26. A	36. C	46. C
7. D	17. B	27. C	37. B	47. D
8. D	18. C	28. C	38. C	48. B
9. B	19. C	29. D	39. C	49. C
10. C	20. C	30. D	40. D	50. D

EXAMINATION SECTION
TEST 1

DIRECTIONS: Each question or incomplete statement is followed by several suggested answers or completions. Select the one that BEST answers the question or completes the statement. *PRINT THE LETTER OF THE CORRECT ANSWER IN THE SPACE AT THE RIGHT.*

Questions 1-16.

DIRECTIONS: Questions 1 through 16 are to be answered on the basis of the New York City subway system.

1. A man traveling on the number *4* train may change at Atlantic Avenue to the _____ train.

   A. *A*
   B. *F*
   C. number *6*
   D. number *2*

2. An express station NOT on the *A* line is _____ Street.

   A. 160 B. 175 C. 181 D. 190

3. A *B* train which leaves Brighton Beach at 7:00 P.M. on Monday stops at

   A. Parkside Ave.
   B. Beverley Rd.
   C. Newkirk Plaza
   D. Avenue R

4. There is *D* train service to Coney Island

   A. at no time
   B. all the time
   C. during *off* hours
   D. during *rush* hours

5. The *R* train is scheduled to travel from Woodhaven Boulevard to Whitehall Street in APPROXIMATELY _____ minutes.

   A. 30 B. 40 C. 50 D. 70

6. During A.M. rush hours, Manhattan-bound number *1* trains may skip _____ Street.

   A. 157
   B. 137
   C. 116
   D. this train makes all stops

7. A passenger on the Lexington Avenue local can transfer free to the 6th Avenue local at

   A. 125 Street
   B. Hunts Pt. Ave.
   C. 96 Street
   D. Bleecker Street

8. The BEST way of going to the new Whitney Museum is by means of the

   A. Broadway Local
   B. Eighth Avenue Express
   C. Myrtle Ave. Express
   D. Culver Shuttle

9. The train that makes stops in three different boroughs is the _____ train.

   A. number *4* B. number *1* C. number *7* D. *C*

10. A line that terminates in Queens is the _____ line.

    A. D   B. M   C. number 6   D. number 5

11. A passenger on an *F* train should be able to get off at the Sutphin Blvd. station if the time is

    A. 5 P.M.   B. 6 P.M.   C. 9 P.M.   D. any time

12. The number 5 Lexington Ave. Express includes stops from Bronx Park East to Nereld Ave.

    A. during rush hours only
    B. at night only
    C. at all times
    D. on weekends only

13. A train that is NOT in service all the time is the

    A. *E* train
    B. Lexington Ave. Express
    C. Franklin Ave. Shuttle
    D. *C* train

14. The train which makes the MOST station stops between 59th St. and 125th St. in Manhattan is the _____ train.

    A. D   B. A   C. C   D. number 1

15. On a Saturday, a passenger on the *A* train can transfer at 59th St.-Columbus Circle to the

    A. *C* train
    B. *D* train
    C. *B* train
    D. Flushing Local

16. On a Sunday, a passenger at the Times Square-42nd St. station can transfer from the _____ train to the _____ train.

    A. *A; F*
    B. *B; R*
    C. number 7; number 1
    D. *N; L*

Questions 17-21.

DIRECTIONS: Questions 17 through 21 are to be answered on the basis of the system of signal indications that is used on Division B (previously BMT and IND) and most of Division A (previously IRT).

17. A signal that gives ONLY a stop and stay indication is a(n) _____ signal.

    A. marker   B. dwarf   C. automatic   D. home

18. A signal whose aspect is controlled ONLY by the movement of a train is called a(n) _____ signal.

    A. home   B. automatic   C. marker   D. dwarf

19. The signal aspect which means proceed on main route and be prepared to stop at the next signal is _____ over _____.

   A. green; green
   B. yellow; green
   C. green; yellow
   D. yellow; yellow

20. The signal aspect which indicates that the motorman should stop and operate the automatic stop manual release is _____ over _____.

   A. red; red
   B. yellow; yellow
   C. red; red over yellow
   D. yellow; yellow over yellow

21. The signal aspect which means proceed is

   A. white   B. yellow   C. blue   D. green

22. Triggers and closing caps are used for operating the doors of _____ car(s).

   A. R-1 to R-14
   B. R-15 to R-22
   C. R-26 to R-38
   D. the R-44

23. A conductor is required to report any change of address within _____ days.

   A. two   B. three   C. five   D. seven

24. When a conductor finds that he cannot report for work because of illness, he is required to call in sick prior to reporting time by AT LEAST _____ hour(s).

   A. 1   B. 2   C. 12   D. 24

25. A conductor must report absence due to illness to the

   A. desk trainmaster
   B. terminal dispatcher
   C. motorman
   D. crew dispatcher

26. The TOTAL number of interior and exterior guard lights on a train which is equipped with both types is

   A. 1   B. 2   C. 4   D. 8

27. When there is smoke in the subway, a motorman should radio the

   A. safety supervisor
   B. desk trainmaster
   C. ventilation supervisor
   D. power department supervisor

28. The FIRST light that a flagman should place in its position when he is setting up is the _____ light.

   A. red   B. green   C. white   D. yellow

29. Passengers on R-44 cars are alerted that the doors are being closed by means of a(n)

   A. announcement over the PA system
   B. buzzer
   C. chime
   D. flashing red light

30. The length of the R-44 car is APPROXIMATELY _____ feet.   30.___
    A. 60   B. 65   C. 70   D. 75

KEY (CORRECT ANSWERS)

1.	D	16.	C
2.	A	17.	A
3.	C	18.	B
4.	B	19.	B
5.	C	20.	C
6.	D	21.	D
7.	D	22.	A
8.	B	23.	D
9.	A	24.	A
10.	B	25.	D
11.	D	26.	C
12.	A	27.	B
13.	D	28.	B
14.	D	29.	C
15.	B	30.	D

EXAMINATION SECTION
TEST 1

DIRECTIONS: Each question or incomplete statement is followed by several suggested answers or completions. Select the one that BEST answers the question or completes the statement. *PRINT THE LETTER OF THE CORRECT ANSWER IN THE SPACE AT THE RIGHT.*

1. It is the obligation of each employee to keep his department informed as to his correct name, address, and telephone number.
   Any change of address MUST be reported within

   A. 24 hours   B. 2 days   C. 3 days   D. 1 week

2. When should an on-the-job accident to an employee be reported to his supervisor?

   A. Only if the injury is serious
   B. As soon as possible
   C. After he is treated at the authority clinic
   D. If compensation for injury is called for

3. The PROPER type of firefighting equipment to be used on an electrical fire is a

   A. soda-acid type extinguisher
   B. fire hose and water
   C. dry-chemical type extinguisher
   D. foam type extinguisher

4. Of the following, the BEST reason for conductors to be courteous to passengers is to

   A. discourage vandalism
   B. speed up train operations
   C. maintain good public relations
   D. assure passenger safety

5. The MAIN reason for the authority posting commercial advertisements in subway cars is to

   A. increase the income of the authority
   B. help passengers pass time pleasantly on long runs
   C. make the cars attractive
   D. inform the passengers about good products

6. Of the following, the BEST reason why an employee is required to give his supervisor a written report of an unusual occurrence immediately is that the

   A. report may be too lengthy if the employee has more time for writing it
   B. employee will not be as likely to forget to make the report
   C. supervisor can keep his reports up-to-date
   D. report will tend to be more accurate

7. During the rush hour, a passenger asks a platform conductor for directions. If the conductor is not sure of the right answer, he should

    A. tell the passenger to find a public telephone and call train information
    B. tell the passenger to take the next arriving train and ask that train's conductor
    C. give the passenger directions that he thinks are right as long as he thinks that the passenger is headed in the right direction
    D. tell the passenger he is not sure and suggest that the passenger wait until they can ask the conductor on the next arriving train for the information

8. If a group of teenagers in a subway car is behaving in a disorderly manner, the FIRST thing a conductor should do is to

    A. request the motorman to call the transit police
    B. eject this group from the train
    C. ask this group to quiet down
    D. refuse to leave the station until this group quiets down

Questions 9-11.

DIRECTIONS: Questions 9 through 11 are to be answered on the basis of the Accident Report below. Read this report carefully before answering the questions. Select your answers ONLY on the basis of this report.

ACCIDENT REPORT

On February 14, at 3:45 P.M., Mr. Warren, while on the top of a stairway at the 34th Street Station, realized the D train was in the station loading passengers. In his haste to catch the train, he forcefully ran down the stairs, pushing aside three other people also going down the stairs. Mr. Parker, one of the three people, lost his footing and fell to the bottom of the stairs. Working on the platform, I saw Mr. Parker lose his footing as a result of Mr. Warren's actions, and I immediately went to his aid. Station Supervisor Brown was attracted to the incident after a crowd had gathered. After 15 minutes, the injured man, Mr. Parker, got up and boarded a train that was in the station and, therefore, he was not hurt seriously.

R. Sands #3214
Conductor

9. Since accident reports should only contain facts, which of the following should NOT be put into the accident report?

    A. The incident took place at the 34th Street Station
    B. Mr. Parker was not hurt seriously
    C. The date that the report was written
    D. Mr. Sands went to the aid of the injured man

10. The title of the person submitting the report was

    A. Porter
    B. Assistant Station Supervisor
    C. Conductor
    D. Passenger

11. The TOTAL number of different persons mentioned in this report is 11.____

    A. seven   B. six   C. five   D. four

12. If an employee desires to find out what his general duties and responsibilities are, he should refer to the authority's 12.____

    A. bulletins periodically issued by the operating divisions
    B. schedule of working conditions
    C. book of rules and regulations governing employees
    D. labor relations manual

13. Of the following, the BEST reason for prohibiting the use of intoxicating liquor by employees while on duty is that it may 13.____

    A. make them too active
    B. make them too talkative
    C. impair their job performance
    D. cause them to become ill

14. If a conductor sees a passenger with his feet on a seat, the conductor should 14.____

    A. tell the passenger he will call a transit patrolman
    B. ignore the situation if the car is not crowded
    C. stare at him until he puts his feet on the floor
    D. ask the passenger to please put his feet down

Questions 15-18.

DIRECTIONS: Questions 15 through 18 are to be answered on the basis of the Bulletin printed below. Read this Bulletin carefully before answering the questions. Select your answers ONLY on the basis of this Bulletin.

BULLETIN

Rule 107(m) states, in part, that *Before closing doors, they (Conductors) must afford passengers an opportunity to detrain and entrain....*
    Doors must be left open long enough to allow passengers to enter and exit from the train. Closing doors on passengers too quickly does not help to shorten the station stop and is a violation of the safety and courtesy which must be accorded to all our passengers.
    The proper and effective way to keep passengers moving in and out of the train is to use the public address system. When the train is excessively crowded and passengers on the platform are pushing those in the cars, it may be necessary to close the doors after a reasonable period of time has been allowed. Closing doors on passengers too quickly is a violation of rules and will be cause for disciplinary action.

15. Which of the following statements is CORRECT about closing doors on passengers too quickly? 15.____
    It

    A. will shorten the running time from terminal to terminal
    B. shortens the station stop but is a violation of safety and courtesy
    C. does not help shorten the station stop time
    D. makes the passengers detrain and entrain quicker

16. The BEST way to get passengers to move in and out of cars quickly is to

    A. have the platform conductors urge passengers to move into doorways
    B. make announcements over the public address system
    C. start closing doors while passengers are getting on
    D. set a fixed time for stopping at each station

17. The conductor should leave doors open at each station stop long enough for passengers to

    A. squeeze into an excessively crowded train
    B. get from the local to the express train
    C. get off and get on the train
    D. hear the announcements over the public address system

18. Closing doors on passengers too quickly is a violation of rules and is cause for

    A. the conductor's immediate suspension
    B. the conductor to be sent back to the terminal for another assignment
    C. removal of the conductor at the next station
    D. disciplinary action to be taken against the conductor

Questions 19-21.

DIRECTIONS: Questions 19 through 21 are to be answered SOLELY on the basis of the Bulletin printed below. Read this Bulletin carefully before answering the questions.

BULLETIN

Conductors assigned to train service are not required to wear uniform caps from June 1 to September 30, inclusive.

Conductors assigned to platform duty are required to wear the uniform cap at all times. Conductors are reminded that they must furnish their badge numbers to anyone who requests, same.

During the above-mentioned period, conductors may remove their uniform coats. The regulation summer short-sleeved shirts must be worn with the regulation uniform trousers. Suspenders are not permitted if the uniform coat is removed. Shoes are to be black but sandals, sneakers, suede, canvas, or two-tone footwear must not be worn.

Conductors may work without uniform tie if the uniform coat is removed. However, only the top collar button may be opened. The tie may not be removed if the uniform coat is worn.

19. Conductors assigned to platform duty are required to wear uniform caps

    A. at all times except from June 1 to September 30, inclusive
    B. whenever they are on duty
    C. only from June 1 to September 30, inclusive
    D. only when they remove their uniform coats

20. Suspenders are permitted only if conductors wear

    A. summer short-sleeved shirts with uniform trousers
    B. uniform trousers without belt loops
    C. the type permitted by the authority
    D. uniform coats

21. A conductor must furnish his badge number to

    A. authority supervisors *only*
    B. members of special inspection *only*
    C. anyone who asks him for it
    D. passengers *only*

22. As a train is leaving a station, the conductor notices a passenger being dragged along the platform with his leg caught in a door.
    The FIRST action the conductor should take is to

    A. pull the emergency cord
    B. call the motorman on the public address system
    C. yell to the platform conductor to pull the man away from the door
    D. run to the car door holding this passenger and try to help him

23. If a conductor is about to close the door and he sees a passenger with a folded baby carriage hastening to get on the train, he should

    A. tell the passenger that baby carriages are not allowed on trains
    B. tell the passenger to hurry up
    C. hold the doors open long enough to allow the passenger to get on
    D. hold the doors open no longer than the required 10 seconds

24. An employee must notify his assignment desk or control office that he will be absent because of illness one hour before his reporting time so that

    A. a substitute can be provided if necessary
    B. he can be denied sick leave if his attendance record is poor
    C. his reason for absence can be checked quickly
    D. the timekeeper in the payroll section can be properly notified

25. Kennedy Airport and LaGuardia Airport are both located in Queens.
    Of the following, the CORRECT statement regarding their locations is that

    A. both Kennedy Airport and LaGuardia Airport are in the northern section of Queens
    B. both Kennedy Airport and LaGuardia Airport are in the southern section of Queens
    C. Kennedy Airport is in the southern section of Queens while LaGuardia Airport is in the northern section of Queens
    D. Kennedy Airport is in the northern section of Queens while LaGuardia Airport is in the southern section of Queens

26. Madison Square Garden is at the same general location as

    A. Pennsylvania Station
    B. Rockefeller Center
    C. Battery Park
    D. Grand Central Station

27. A park located in the northeast corner of the Bronx is

    A. St. Mary's Park
    B. Van Cortlandt Park
    C. Crotona Park
    D. Pelham Bay Park

28. The Manhattan terminal of the Staten Island Ferry is located CLOSEST to

   A. Washington Square Park
   B. the Queensboro Bridge
   C. the World Trade Center
   D. Union Square

29. Two points of interest located in the Bronx are

   A. the New York Aquarium and the Hall of Fame
   B. Orchard Beach and the New York Botanical Garden
   C. Van Cortlandt Park and Citi Field
   D. City Island and Grant's Tomb

30. Of the following, the one which is located south of 42nd Street in Manhattan is the

   A. Rockefeller Center
   B. United Nations Assembly Building
   C. Inwood Hill Park
   D. Empire State Building

KEY (CORRECT ANSWERS)

1.	D	16.	B
2.	B	17.	C
3.	C	18.	D
4.	C	19.	B
5.	A	20.	D
6.	D	21.	C
7.	D	22.	A
8.	C	23.	C
9.	B	24.	A
10.	C	25.	C
11.	B	26.	A
12.	C	27.	D
13.	C	28.	C
14.	D	29.	B
15.	C	30.	D

TEST 2

DIRECTIONS: Each question or incomplete statement is followed by several suggested answers or completions. Select the one that BEST answers the question or completes the statement. *PRINT THE LETTER OF THE CORRECT ANSWER IN THE SPACE AT THE RIGHT.*

Questions 1-3.

DIRECTIONS: Questions 1 through 3 are to be answered on the basis of the following Directive. Read this Directive carefully before answering these questions. Select your answer ONLY on the basis of this Directive.

DIRECTIVE

When work trains having miscellaneous equipment (flat cars, crane cars, etc.) are in transit, the following flagging and safety instructions must be adhered to:

1. When flat cars are at the forward end of a train, the Flagman will station himself on the leading car. The Flagman will keep in constant communication with the Train Operator through the use of sound-powered telephones. If sound-powered telephones become defective and alternate means of communications are needed, the Command Center must be called for instructions. Positive communications must be maintained while the train is in motion. Any loss of communication will be a signal for the Train Operator to *Stop and Investigate.*

2. When flat cars are trailing, the Flagman will station himself on the rear of the last motor car in a position to view the trailing cars. Flagmen must observe that tail lights are illuminated at all times.

3. At all times when these trains are stopped for any reason, the Train Operator must sound two blasts of the whistle or horn before proceeding.

4. Safety demands that Train Operators and Flagmen investigate all causes of a train going into emergency, particularly when an employee is known to be riding a flat car.

5. Under no circumstances will an employee walk across a flat car while a train is in motion.

1. When flat cars are at the forward end of a work train, the Flagman will station himself

   A. at the rear of the last motor car
   B. on the trailing flat car
   C. on the leading flat car
   D. at the front of the first motor car

2. When a train with flat cars has stopped and the Train Operator wishes to proceed again, he MUST

   A. call the Command Center
   B. shout instructions to the Flagman
   C. check that the Flagman is using the correct signals
   D. sound two blasts of the whistle or horn

3. When there is a loss of positive communication between the Train Operator and the Flagman while the train is in motion, the Train Operator should

   A. tell the Flagman to use his flashlight for flagging
   B. stop the train and investigate the situation
   C. tell the Flagman to use hand signals for flagging
   D. put the train into emergency

4. A conductor earns $21.64 per hour. He is paid time and one-half for each hour worked over 40 hours per week. If a conductor works 44 hours in one week, his gross salary for that week is

   A. $995.36   B. $995.44   C. $999.44   D. $999.84

Questions 5-12.

DIRECTIONS: Questions 5 through 12 are to be answered on the basis of the Weekday Train Schedule for the Dumont Line below. In answering these questions, refer ONLY to this schedule.

WEEKDAY TRAIN SCHEDULE - DUMONT LINE

Train #	EASTBOUND			Magic Mall		WESTBOUND		
	Harvard Square Leave	Pleasure Plaza Leave	Harding Street Leave	Arr.	Lv.	Harding Street Leave	Pleasure Plaza Leave	Harvard Square Arrive
69	7:48	7:51	7:56	8:00	8:06	8:10	8:15	8:18
70	7:54	7:57	8:02	8:06	8:12	8:16	8:21	8:24
71	8:00	8:03	8:08	8:12	8:18	8:22	8:27	8:30
72	8:04	8:07	8:13	8:17	8:22	8:26	8:31	8:34
73	8:08	8:11	8:17	8:21	8:26	8:30	8:35	8:38
74	8:12	8:15	8:20	8:24	8:30	8:34	8:39	8:42
75	8:16	8:19	8:24	8:28	8:34	8:38	8:43	8:46
69	8:20	8:23	8:28	8:32	8:38	8:42	8:47	8:50
70	8:26	8:29	8:34	8:38	8:44	8:48	8:53	8:56

5. Train #70 is scheduled to leave Pleasure Plaza on its second westbound trip to Harvard Square at

   A. 7:57   B. 8:21   C. 8:29   D. 8:53

6. The time it should take Train #74 to go from Harvard Square to Magic Mall is _____ minutes.

   A. 8   B. 12   C. 18   D. 30

7. As shown on this schedule, the number of trains arriving at Magic Mall and standing there for less than 6 minutes before leaving is

   A. 0   B. 2   C. 7   D. 9

8. The number of trains shown on the schedule having different train numbers is

   A. 6   B. 7   C. 8   D. 9

9. Going towards Harvard Square, Train #71 is scheduled to leave Pleasure Plaza at   9._____

   A. 8:03   B. 8:18   C. 8:27   D. 8:30

10. Passengers boarding at Harding Street and wishing to get to Harvard Square by 8:45   10._____
    would have to board a train which is scheduled to leave Magic Mall no later than

    A. 8:26   B. 8:30   C. 8:34   D. 8:38

11. Train #73 should leave Harding Street on its eastbound trip _____ minutes after leaving   11._____
    Harvard Square.

    A. 7   B. 8   C. 9   D. 10

12. Due to door trouble, Train #72 (eastbound) is turned at Harding Street when it was   12._____
    scheduled to leave, and this operation takes 5 minutes.
    Since the running time for the return trip back to Harvard Square is the same time as
    that for the eastbound trip, it should arrive back at Harvard Square at

    A. 8:22   B. 8:27   C. 8:31   D. 8:39

13. If a train comes to a sudden stop and there is a delay in proceeding, the conductor   13._____
    should explain the reason for the delay to the passengers in order to

    A. prevent them from blaming the train crew
    B. prevent them from going on the track
    C. keep them informed and calm
    D. get them to help each other

14. Recently, the authority instituted a program of closing off the rear portion of subway   14._____
    trains between the hours of 8 P.M. and 4 A.M.
    This was done MAINLY to

    A. ease the job of the conductor
    B. cut down on the number of people needed to operate trains
    C. allow necessary repairs to be made in the closed-off cars
    D. attempt to cut down on crime in the subways.

4 (#2)

Questions 15-19.

DIRECTIONS: Questions 15 through 19 are to be answered on the basis of the Broad Street Line timetable printed on the next page. The numbers represent the total time (in minutes) that it takes the Broad Street Line local and express trains to travel from Frankford Avenue to the stations listed. The running times shown on the table include station-stop times. When answering these questions, use this timetable.

BROAD STREET LINE

Stations	Total Running Times, In Minutes	
	Local	Express
Frankford Avenue	-	-
Columbus Street	7	-
Overland Parkway	12 1/2	10
Victoria Boulevard	15	-
Market Street	17	14
Prince Street	24	-
Kings Avenue	28	-
Elizabeth Drive	33	28
Paradox Place	35	-
Del Prado Parkway	38 1/2	33
Monroe Avenue	44	-
McKinley Plaza	48	41

15. Both an express train and local train are standing in the Market Street Station. If both trains leave Market Street at the same time, how many minutes would a rider SAVE by using an express train in traveling to Del Prado Parkway?

    A. 1 1/2   B. 2 1/2   C. 3 1/2   D. 4 1/2

16. If a Broad Street local train leaves Columbus Street at 8:10 P.M., it should arrive at Monroe Avenue at _____ P.M.

    A. 8:22   B. 8:34   C. 8:41   D. 8:47

17. A passenger takes a local train from Columbus Street to Overland Parkway and then an express train from Overland Parkway to McKinley Plaza.
    Assuming no waiting time at any station, the TOTAL trip should take _____ minutes.

    A. 36 1/2   B. 43 1/2   C. 46 1/2   D. 51 1/2

18. A Broad Street local leaves Frankford Avenue at 9:15 A.M. A Broad Street express leaves Frankford Avenue at 9:18 A.M.
    At what station will the express meet the local?

    A. Overland Parkway   B. Market Street
    C. Elizabeth Drive   D. Del Prado Parkway

19. A conductor on the Broad Street Line is scheduled to make three roundtrips on the local train between Frankford Avenue and McKinley Plaza with a 6-minute layover at these two terminal stations.
    What is the TOTAL running time, including time for layovers?
    _____ hours and _____ minutes.

    A. 4; 30   B. 4; 36   C. 5; 18   D. 5; 24

20. A woman passenger complains to a platform conductor that a public telephone in the station is not working and that she lost 20 cents in trying to use it.
The conductor should tell her to

   A. contact the telephone subdivision of the maintenance of way department
   B. complain to the railroad clerk on duty in the change booth
   C. contact the telephone company for a refund
   D. make a complaint to a transit patrolman

20.____

21. A transportation authority institutes a half-fare program on Sundays.
The MAIN purpose for this type of program is to

   A. decrease the number of riders on buses and trains on Sundays
   B. get more people to use trains and buses on Sundays
   C. encourage people to visit points of interest in the city
   D. find out if the fare should also be reduced during the week

21.____

22. If a conductor reads a bulletin which he doesn't understand, the BEST thing for him to do is to

   A. try to follow the directions in the bulletin as well as he can
   B. discuss the bulletin with other conductors
   C. ask the motorman of his train for an explanation
   D. ask his supervisor what the bulletin means

22.____

23. In order to be granted a paid or unpaid leave of absence on account of illness, an employee MUST file a written application, using the proper forms, within _____ after his return to work

   A. 24 hours   B. 2 days   C. 3 days   D. 1 week

23.____

24. A person has fallen on the subway station platform and says he has broken his leg.
While waiting for an ambulance, the platform conductor should

   A. help him over to a bench while putting as little weight as possible on the injured leg
   B. make him as comfortable as possible without moving him
   C. examine him for other possible injuries
   D. apply a tourniquet to his leg from a first aid kit

24.____

25. Smoking in subway cars is prohibited MAINLY because it can

   A. endanger a smoker's health
   B. cause fires
   C. bother passengers
   D. cause cars to be littered with cigarette butts

25.____

KEY (CORRECT ANSWERS)

1.	C	11.	C
2.	D	12.	B
3.	B	13.	C
4.	B	14.	D
5.	D	15.	B
6.	B	16.	D
7.	B	17.	A
8.	B	18.	B
9.	C	19.	C
10.	B	20.	C

21. B
22. D
23. C
24. B
25. B

TEST 3

DIRECTIONS: Each question or incomplete statement is followed by several suggested answers or completions. Select the one that BEST answers the question or completes the statement. *PRINT THE LETTER OF THE CORRECT ANSWER IN THE SPACE AT THE RIGHT.*

1. Making an emergency stop of a subway train should be avoided if possible MAINLY because it might cause 1.____

   A. passengers to be late for work
   B. a train derailment
   C. hard wear on brakes and rails
   D. injuries to passengers

Questions 2-3.

DIRECTIONS: Questions 2 and 3 are to be answered SOLELY on the basis of the following Bulletin.

BULLETIN

Effective immediately, Conductors on trains equipped with public address systems shall make the following announcements in addition to their regular station announcement. At stations where passengers normally board trains from their homes or places of employment, the announcement shall be *Good Morning* or *Good Afternoon* or *Good Evening,* depending on the time of the day. At stations where passengers normally leave trains for their homes or places of employment, the announcement shall be *Have a Good Day* or *Good Night,* depending on the time of day or night.

2. The MAIN purpose of making the additional announcements mentioned in the Bulletin is MOST likely to 2.____

   A. keep passengers informed about the time of day
   B. determine whether the public address system works in case of an emergency
   C. make the passengers' ride more pleasant
   D. have the conductor get used to using the public address system

3. According to this Bulletin, a conductor should greet passengers boarding the *D* train at the Coney Island Station at 8 A.M. Monday by announcing 3.____

   A. Have a Good Day
   B. Good Morning
   C. Watch your step as you leave
   D. Good Evening

4. A passenger who seems to be drunk, but has not disturbed anyone, sits down on a seat near the conductor's cab. 4.____
   Of the following, the BEST way for the conductor to handle this situation is to

   A. gently lead this passenger off the train at the next station
   B. pay no attention to this passenger
   C. contact the transit police and ask them to remove this passenger
   D. do nothing but check frequently to see if this passenger starts to annoy anyone

5. Of the following, the BEST way for a conductor to keep informed of the latest changes in work procedures is to

    A. read all the new bulletins when he signs in
    B. study the book of rules
    C. ask the other conductors
    D. depend on his supervisor to tell him

6. The statistics compiled by the safety bureau of the subway system indicate that one out of every ten employees is qualified to give first aid and that one out of every five employees met with an accident during the past year.
Of the following, the ONLY CORRECT statement that can be made from these figures for the past year is:

    A. One-half of the accidents occurred without a qualified employee present who was able to give first aid
    B. There would be fewer accidents if there were more employees trained to give first aid
    C. The number of accidents was twice the number of employees qualified to give first aid
    D. Each qualified employee gave first aid to two employees who had met with accidents

7. A conductor has just finished his tour of duty. As he is leaving the terminal, he finds a portion of the station platform has become slippery as a result of an oil spill. Which of the following is the BEST action for the conductor to take?

    A. Write a report to his supervisor about the condition of the platform.
    B. Warn any other employees that he sees before leaving about the condition of the platform.
    C. Report the condition of the platform to his supervisor when he sees him.
    D. Contact his supervisor about the condition of the platform before leaving the station.

8. While you are working as a conductor on a train, a friend of yours boards the train and tries to engage you in a long conversation.
You should

    A. continue the conversation only between stations
    B. suggest that your friend talk to you only in the conductor's cab
    C. tell your friend that private conversations are not allowed while you are working
    D. request your friend to go into another car

9. An employee using his travel pass to ride the subway MUST

    A. report any unusual occurrences to his supervisor
    B. report it as stolen to the transit police if he loses it
    C. stand if there are not enough seats for revenue passengers
    D. notify the conductor that he is on the train and available for assistance in case of an emergency

10. Employers are often requested to arrange for *staggered working hours* for their employees in order to

    A. increase the revenue obtained by the subway system
    B. allow a husband and wife in a family to work different hours in order to care for the children
    C. reduce rush hour crowding in the subways
    D. give employees more time to shop when the department stores are open

11. The maximum number of cars which can be used on a subway train depends MAINLY on the

    A. length of station platforms in the subway system
    B. number of drive motors in each subway car
    C. headway between trains during rush hours
    D. number of matched pairs of new-type subway cars making up the train

12. If a platform conductor sees an armed robber *mugging* a passenger, he should

    A. run up to the street and look for help
    B. look for a weapon to attack the robber
    C. call on other passengers to help him catch the robber
    D. quickly contact the nearest transit patrolman

13. A *B* train which leaves Brighton Beach at 11:00 A.M. stops at

    A. Prospect Avenue
    B. Union Street
    C. 9th Street
    D. DeKalb Avenue

14. An express transfer station on the Lexington Avenue local is

    A. 33rd Street
    B. Astor Place
    C. 86th Street
    D. 96th Street

15. A passenger at the West 4th Street Station on the *A* line can transfer to the _____ line.

    A. *L*   B. *Q*   C. *N*   D. *F*

16. The BEST way to go to Grant's Tomb is by means of the _____ train.

    A. *A*   B. Number *1*   C. Number *4*   D. *D*

17. A passenger at the Coney Island-Stillwell Avenue Station on the *F* line wishes to transfer to the *A* line.
    The NEAREST transfer point is

    A. West 4th Street
    B. Church Avenue
    C. Jay Street-MetroTech
    D. Bergen Street

18. An express station on the Number *3* line is

    A. 50th Street
    B. 59th Street-Columbus Circle
    C. 72nd Street
    D. Winthrop Street

19. The *G* train travels between Court Square and Church Avenue stations

    A. all the time
    B. at no time
    C. during *rush* hours
    D. during *off* hours

20. A passenger on the Number *1* Broadway local train can transfer FREE to the *A* train at which of the following stations?

    A. Cathedral Parkway (110th Street)
    B. 59th Street - Columbus Circle
    C. Chambers Street
    D. Penn Station - 34th Street

21. To visit the Cloisters, the BEST way is to a station on the _____ line.

    A. *A*   B. Number *1*   C. Number *3*   D. *D*

22. A line that is in service during rush hours ONLY is the

    A. *A* line
    B. Franklin Ave. shuttle
    C. *C* line
    D. *E* line

23. A train that makes stops in Manhattan and the Bronx ONLY is the _____ train.

    A. Number *1*   B. *B*   C. *F*   D. *J*

24. A train that makes stops ONLY in Manhattan is the _____ train.

    A. *A*
    B. *E*
    C. *M*
    D. None of the above

25. The *L* train is scheduled to travel from Rockaway Parkway to 8th Avenue in APPROXIMATELY _____ minutes.

    A. 60   B. 50   C. 40   D. 25

KEY (CORRECT ANSWERS)

1. D
2. C
3. B
4. D
5. A

6. C
7. D
8. C
9. C
10. C

11. A
12. D
13. D
14. C
15. D

16. B
17. C
18. C
19. A
20. B

21. A
22. C
23. A
24. D
25. C

READING COMPREHENSION
UNDERSTANDING AND INTERPRETING WRITTEN MATERIAL

EXAMINATION SECTION
TEST 1

DIRECTIONS: Each question or incomplete statement is followed by several suggested answers or completions. Select the one that BEST answers the question or completes the statement. *PRINT THE LETTER OF THE CORRECT ANSWER IN THE SPACE AT THE RIGHT.*

Questions 1-10.

DIRECTIONS: Questions 1 through 10 are to be answered on the basis of the description of an incident given below. Read the description carefully before answering these questions.

DESCRIPTION OF INCIDENT

On Tuesday, October 8, at about 4:00 P.M., bus operator Sam Bell, Badge No. 3871, whose accident record was perfect, was operating his half-filled bus, No. 4392Y, northbound and on schedule along Dean Street. At this time, a male passenger who was apparently intoxicated started to yell and to use loud and profane language. The bus driver told this passenger to be quiet or to get off the bus. The passenger said that he would not be quiet but indicated that he wanted to get off the bus by moving toward the front door exit. When he reached the front of the bus, which at the time was in motion, the intoxicated passenger slapped the bus operator on the back and pulled the steering wheel sharply. This action caused the bus to sideswipe a passenger automobile coming from the opposite direction before the operator could stop the bus. The sideswiped car was a red 2007 Pontiac 2-door convertible, License 6416-KN, driven by Albert Holt. The bus driver kept the doors of his bus closed and blew the horn vigorously. The horn blowing was quickly answered as Sergeant Henry Burns, Badge No. 1208, and Patrolman Joe Cross, Badge No. 24643, happened to be following a few cars behind the bus in police car No. 736. The intoxicated passenger, who gave his name as John Doe, was placed under arrest, and Patrolman Cross took the names of witnesses while Sergeant Burns recorded the necessary vehicular information. Investigation showed that no one was injured in the accident and that the entire damage to the automobile was having its side slightly pushed in.

1. From the information given, it can be reasoned that

    A. it was just beginning to rain
    B. Dean Street is a two-way street
    C. there were mostly women shoppers on the bus
    D. most seats in the bus were filled

2. The name of the policeman who was riding in the police car with the sergeant was

    A. Cross   B. Bell   C. Holt   D. Burns

3. From the description, it is evident that the passenger automobile was traveling   3.____

   A. north B. south C. east D. west

4. It is logical to conclude that the passenger automobile was damaged on its   4.____

   A. front end B. rear end
   C. right side D. left side

5. A fact concerning the intoxicated passenger that is clearly stated in the above description is that he   5.____

   A. was intoxicated when he got on the bus
   B. hit a fellow passenger
   C. pulled the steering wheel sharply
   D. was not arrested

6. The bus operator called the attention of the police by   6.____

   A. sideswiping an oncoming car
   B. yelling and using profane language
   C. blowing his horn vigorously
   D. stopping a police car coming from the opposite direction

7. A reasonable conclusion that can be drawn from the above description is that   7.____

   A. the name John Doe was fictitious
   B. the sideswiped automobile was from out of town
   C. some of the passengers on the bus were injured
   D. the bus operator tried to put the intoxicated passenger off the bus

8. The number of the police car involved in the incident was   8.____

   A. 4392Y B. 6416-KN C. 1208 D. 736

9. From the facts stated, it is obvious that the bus operator was   9.____

   A. behind schedule
   B. driving too close to the center of the street
   C. discourteous to the intoxicated passenger
   D. a good driver

10. It is clearly stated that the   10.____

    A. sideswiped automobile was a blue sedan
    B. bus driver kept the bus doors closed until the police came
    C. incident happened on a Thursday
    D. police sergeant took down the names of witnesses

Questions 11-20.

DIRECTIONS: Questions 11 through 20 are to be answered on the basis of the paragraph below covering cleaning supplies. Refer to this paragraph when answering these questions.

A Note from Mel

Deal Breakers
No Marriage
No Smoking
Consistency
Honesty

Milk
Bread
Deli Meat
Napkins
Chicken

520 445 3750

Bi-Weekly 13/14

LocusValley 106/107

Exit 50 Expressway

CLEANING SUPPLIES

Certain amounts of cleaning supplies are used each week at each station of the Transit Authority. The following information applies to a station of average size. For cleaning floors, tiles, and toilets, approximately 14 pounds of soap powder is used each week. A scouring powder is used to clean unusually difficult stains, and approximately 1 1/2 pounds is used in a week. A disinfectant solution is used for cleaning telephone alcoves, toilets, and booth floors, and approximately 1 quart of undiluted disinfectant is used each week. To make a regular strength disinfectant solution, 1/4 ounce of undiluted disinfectant is added to 14 gallons of water. One pint of lemon oil is used each week to polish metal surfaces in booths and in other station areas.

11. In a period of 4 weeks, the amount of soap powder that is used at the average station is MOST NEARLY _____ pounds.

    A. 48   B. 52   C. 56   D. 60

12. In a period of 1 year, the amount of scouring powder that is used at the average station is MOST NEARLY _____ pounds.

    A. 26   B. 52   C. 64   D. 78

13. If a certain large station uses 1 1/2 times the soap powder that an average station uses, then the larger station uses MOST NEARLY _____ pounds a week.

    A. 14   B. 21   C. 24   D. 28

14. To make a regular strength disinfectant solution, the number of ounces of undiluted disinfectant that should be added to 3 gallons of water is

    A. 4   B. 3/4   C. 1   D. 1 1/4

15. To make a double strength disinfectant solution, the number of ounces of undiluted disinfectant that should be added to 3 gallons of water is

    A. 4   B. 3/4   C. 1   D. 1 1/2

16. In a period of 4 weeks, the amount of lemon oil that is used at the average station is _____ gallon(s).

    A. 1/4   B. 4   C. 1   D. 1 1/2

17. In a period of one year, the amount of soap powder that is used at 5 average stations is MOST NEARLY _____ pounds.

    A. 260   B. 728   C. 3,640   D. 5,260

18. To clean a station that is difficult to remove, it would be BEST for a porter to use

    A. soap powder   B. scouring powder
    C. disinfectant solution   D. lemon oil

19. Lemon oil should be used for

    A. scouring
    B. regular cleaning
    C. polishing metal surfaces
    D. disinfecting

20. If a smaller than average station uses 3/4 of the amount of scouring powder than an average station uses, then in one week the amount of scouring powder used at the smaller station is MOST NEARLY _____ pound(s).

    A. 7/8   B. 1   C. 1 1/8   D. 1 1/4

Questions 21-25.

DIRECTIONS: Questions 21 through 25, inclusive, are to be answered on the basis of the bus cleaning instructions below, which should be performed in the order given. Read the instructions carefully before answering these questions.

1. SPRAY wheels and mud guards with hand water hose to remove loose dirt.
2. SCRUB mud guards with brush and cleaner.
3. SCRUB wheels with brush and cleaner.
4. SCRAPE grease from wheels with hand scraper.
5. RINSE wheels and mud guards with hand water hose.

21. The cleaning instructions which involve the same parts of the bus are

    A. 1 and 2   B. 1 and 3   C. 2 and 4   D. 1 and 5

22. The scraping takes place

    A. *after* both the spraying and rinsing
    B. *after* the rinsing but before the scrubbing
    C. *before* both the scrubbing and rinsing
    D. *before* the rinsing but after the spraying

23. The hand water hose is NOT used to remove the grease because water

    A. cannot remove the grease properly
    B. would injure the motor
    C. has to be used as cleaner solution
    D. is used only for spraying

24. The brush is used in connection with operations

    A. 1 and 2   B. 2 and 3   C. 3 and 4   D. 4 and 5

25. Loose dirt is removed by

    A. scraping   B. scrubbing   C. spraying   D. rinsing

KEY (CORRECT ANSWERS)

1. B
2. A
3. B
4. D
5. C

6. C
7. A
8. D
9. D
10. B

11. C
12. D
13. B
14. A
15. C

16. B
17. C
18. B
19. C
20. C

21. D
22. D
23. A
24. B
25. C

TEST 2

DIRECTIONS: Each question or incomplete statement is followed by several suggested answers or completions. Select the one that BEST answers the question or completes the statement. *PRINT THE LETTER OF THE CORRECT ANSWER IN THE SPACE AT THE RIGHT.*

Questions 1-8.

DIRECTIONS: Questions 1 through 8 are to be answered on the basis of the information contained in the safety rules given. Read these rules carefully before answering these questions.

SAFETY RULES FOR EMPLOYEES WORKING ON TRACKS

Always carry a hand lantern whenever walking a track and walk opposite to the direction of the traffic on that particular track, if possible.

At all times when walking track, take note of and be prepared to use the spaces available for safety, clear of passing trains. Be careful to avoid those positions where clearance is insufficient.

Employees are particularly cautioned with respect to sections of track on which regular operation of passenger trains may at times be abandoned and which are used as lay-up tracks. Such tracks are likely to be used at any and irregular times by special trains such as work trains, lay-up trains, etc. At no time can any section of track be assumed to be definitely out of service, and employees must observe, when on or near tracks, the usual precautions regardless of any assumption as to operating schedules.

1. Safety rules are MOST useful because they 1._____
    - A. make it unnecessary to think
    - B. prevent carelessness
    - C. are a guide to avoid common dangers
    - D. make the workman responsible for any accident

2. A trackman walking a section of track should walk 2._____
    - A. to the left of the tracks
    - B. to the right of the tracks
    - C. in the direction of traffic
    - D. opposite to the direction of traffic

3. One precaution a trackman should ALWAYS take is to 3._____
    - A. have power turned off on those tracks where he is walking
    - B. place a red lantern behind him when walking back
    - C. wave his lantern constantly when walking track
    - D. note nearby safety spaces

4. Special trains are GENERALLY 4.____

   A. passenger trains on regular schedule
   B. express trains on local tracks
   C. work trains or lay-up trains
   D. trains going opposite to traffic

5. A trackman walking track should 5.____

   A. stay clear of all safety spaces
   B. expect all trains to be on schedule
   C. avoid tracks used by passenger trains
   D. carry a hand lantern

6. On sections of track not used for regular passenger trains, a trackman should 6.____

   A. follow the rules governing tracks in passenger train operation
   B. assume that no trains will be operating
   C. walk in the direction of traffic
   D. disregard the usual precautions

7. Safety spaces are provided in the subway for 7.____

   A. lay-up trains   B. passing trains
   C. employee's use   D. easier walking

8. A trackman would NOT expect lay-up tracks to be used by 8.____

   A. special trains
   B. trains carrying passengers
   C. work trains
   D. lay-up trains

Questions 9-17.

DIRECTIONS: Questions 9 through 17 are to be answered on the basis of the porters' instructions given below. Read these instructions carefully before answering these questions

PORTERS' INSTRUCTIONS

Railroad porters are prohibited from entering the token booths except for cleaning or relieving the railroad clerk. When the cleaning or relief has been completed, porters must leave booths immediately and must not loiter in or around the booths. Porters must not leave their equipment or supplies, such as dust pans, brooms, soap, etc., on any stairway, passageway, walkway, or in any place which may result in a hazard to passengers or others. Whenever an accident occurs on the station where the porter is assigned, he must submit a report on the prescribed form, always giving the condition of the place where the accident occurred. Porters must be in prescribed uniforms ready for work when reporting *on* and *off* duty.

9. The instructions would indicate that the porters' PRINCIPAL duty is to

   A. make out accident reports
   B. wear a uniform
   C. relieve the railroad clerk
   D. keep the station clean

10. Porters are permitted to enter token booths

    A. any time they wish
    B. after finishing cleaning
    C. to relieve the railroad clerk
    D. to avoid loitering elsewhere

11. The PROBABLE reason why porters cannot stay in the token booth even if their regular work is done is because

    A. they have a regular porters' room
    B. they are not trusted
    C. there is no room
    D. passengers may complain

12. Porters are used to relieve railroad clerks MAINLY because

    A. they need the training
    B. they are conveniently available
    C. their regular work is hard
    D. their work is similar

13. In submitting a report on an accident, the porter is instructed to

    A. explain the cause
    B. use any convenient paper
    C. give the condition of the place
    D. telephone it to his superior

14. The MOST likely reason for having special uniforms for porters is to

    A. give them authority
    B. avoid a variety of unpresentable clothes
    C. save them money
    D. permit them to enter without paying fare

15. Evidently, porters must be careful where they leave their equipment or supplies to avoid

    A. spoilage
    B. theft
    C. loss of time
    D. injury to passengers

16. Such instructions to porters are NECESSARY because

    A. there is no other way to do the work
    B. it creates respect for authority
    C. it avoids misunderstandings
    D. they are not expected to think

17. A porter need NOT be in uniform when

    A. doing dirty work
    B. on his day off
    C. reporting *off* duty
    D. relieving the railroad clerk

Questions 18-25.

DIRECTIONS: Questions 18 through 25 are to be answered on the basis of the information contained in the safety rules given below. Read these rules carefully before answering these questions.

TRACKMEN SAFETY RULES ON EMERGENCY ALARM SYSTEM

In case of an emergency requiring the removal of high voltage power from the contact rail, any trackman seeing such emergency shall immediately operate the nearest emergency alarm box, and then immediately use the emergency telephone alongside the box to notify the trainmaster of the nature of the trouble. High voltage will be turned on again only by telephone order from an employee specifically having such authority. The location of this equipment along the trackway is indicated by a blue light. Trackmen are required to know the location of such boxes and the procedure to follow in order to have high voltage contact rail power removed on sections of elevated structure trackway which may not be equipped with emergency alarm boxes.

18. The location of an emergency alarm box is indicated by a(n) _____ light.

    A. red   B. orange   C. green   D. blue

19. Operating an emergency alarm box

    A. calls the fire department
    B. removes power
    C. lights a blue light
    D. restores power

20. All trackmen

    A. have the authority to have power restored
    B. should know the location of emergency alarm boxes
    C. must call the trainmaster before operating an emergency alarm box
    D. do not have the right to operate an emergency alarm box

21. On a track having trains in operation, a nearby emergency alarm box would PROBABLY be operated if

    A. an employee cuts his hand
    B. the emergency telephone rings
    C. the blue light goes on
    D. a break is found in a running track rail

22. After operating an emergency alarm box, the trackman should use the emergency telephone immediately to speak to

    A. his supervisor
    B. the trainmaster
    C. the station agent
    D. his co-workers

23. It would be MOST important to have power restored as quickly as possible in order to reduce

    A. power waste
    B. train damage
    C. train delays
    D. fire hazard

24. If there are no emergency alarm boxes along a trackway, trackmen

    A. cannot have power shut off
    B. are not required to act in an emergency
    C. can have power shut off by following the proper procedure
    D. are forbidden to use the emergency telephone

25. On elevated structure trackways,

    A. emergency alarm boxes may not be found
    B. train delays never occur
    C. the trainmaster is not notified on power removal
    D. power is never removed

KEY (CORRECT ANSWERS)

1. C		11. A	
2. D		12. B	
3. D		13. C	
4. C		14. B	
5. D		15. D	
6. A		16. C	
7. C		17. B	
8. B		18. D	
9. D		19. B	
10. C		20. B	

21. D
22. B
23. C
24. C
25. A

TEST 3

DIRECTIONS: Each question or incomplete statement is followed by several suggested answers or completions. Select the one that BEST answers the question or completes the statement. *PRINT THE LETTER OF THE CORRECT ANSWER IN THE SPACE AT THE RIGHT.*

Questions 1-5.

DIRECTIONS: Questions 1 through 5 are to be answered on the basis of the paragraphs shown below covering the supply duties of assistant station supervisors. Refer to these paragraphs when answering these questions.

SUPPLY DUTIES OF ASSISTANT STATION SUPERVISORS

The assistant station supervisors on the 8 A.M. to 4 P.M. tour will be responsible for the ordering of porter cleaning supplies and will inventory individual stations under their jurisdiction in order to maintain the necessary supplies to insure proper sanitary standards. They will be responsible not only for the ordering of such supplies but will see to it that ordered supplies are distributed as required in accordance with order supply sheets. Assistant station supervisors on the 4 P.M. to 12 Midnight and 12 Midnight to 8 A.M. shift will cooperate with the A.M. station supervisor to properly control supplies.

The 4 P.M. to 12 Midnight assistant station supervisors will be responsible for the ordering and control of all stationery supplies used by railroad clerks in the performance of their duties. They will also see that supplies are kept in a neat and orderly manner. The assistant station supervisors in charge of *Supply Storerooms* will see to it that material so ordered will be given to the porters for delivery to the respective booths. Cooperation of all supervision applies in this instance.

The 12 Midnight to 8 A.M. assistant station supervisors will be responsible for the storing of materials delivered by special work train (sawdust, etc.). They will also see that all revenue bags which are torn, dirty, etc. are picked up and sent to the field office for delivery to the bag room.

Any supplies needed other than those distributed on regular supply days will be requested by submitting a requisition to the supply control desk for emergency delivery.

1. The assistant station supervisors who are responsible for ordering all stationery supplies used by railroad clerks are the ones on the _____ tour.   1._____

    A. 8 A.M. to 4 P.M.
    B. 4 P.M. to 12 Midnight
    C. 12 Midnight to 8 A.M.
    D. 4 P.M. to 2 P.M.

2. Storing of materials delivered by special work trains is the responsibility of assistant station supervisors on the _____ tour.   2._____

    A. 8 A.M. to 4 P.M.
    B. 4 P.M. to 12 Midnight
    C. 12 Midnight to 8 A.M.
    D. 4 P.M. to 2 P.M.

3. Torn revenue bags should be picked up and sent FIRST to

   A. the bag room
   B. the supply control desk
   C. a supply storeroom
   D. the field office

4. To obtain an emergency delivery of supplies on a day other than a regular supply day, a requisition should be submitted to the

   A. appropriate zone office
   B. appropriate field office
   C. supply control desk
   D. station supervisor

5. The assistant station supervisor responsible for ordering porter cleaning supplies will inventory individual stations PRIMARILY for the end purpose of

   A. insuring proper sanitary standards
   B. maintaining necessary supplies
   C. keeping track of supplies
   D. distributing supplies fairly

Questions 6-10.

DIRECTIONS: Questions 6 through 10 are to be answered on the basis of the paragraphs shown below entitled POSTING OF DIVERSION OF SERVICE NOTICES. Refer to these paragraphs when answering these questions.

POSTING OF DIVERSION OF SERVICE NOTICES

The following procedures concerning the receiving and posting of service diversion notices will be strictly adhered to:

Assistant station supervisors who receive notices will sign a receipt and return it to the Station Department Office. It will be their responsibility to ensure that all notices are posted at affected stations and a notation made in the transmittal logs. All excess notices will be tied and a notation made thereon, indicating the stations and the date notices were posted, and the name and pass number of the assistant station supervisor posting same. The word *EXCESS* is to be boldly written on bundled notices and the bundle placed in a conspicuous location. When loose notices, without any notations, are discovered in any field office, assistant station supervisor's office, or other Station Department locations, the matter is to be thoroughly investigated to make sure proper distribution has been completed. All stations where a diversion of service exists must be contacted daily by the assistant station supervisor covering that group and hour to ensure that a sufficient number of notices are posted and employees are aware of the situation. In any of the above circumstances, notation is to be made in the supervisory log. Station supervisors will be responsible for making certain all affected stations in their respective groups have notices posted and for making spot checks each day diversions are in effect.

6. An assistant station supervisor who has signed a receipt upon receiving service diversion notices must return the

   A. notice to the Station Department office
   B. receipt to the Station Department office
   C. receipt and the transmittal log to the affected stations
   D. transmittal log after making a notation in it

7. Of the following, the information which is NOT required to be written on a bundle of excess notices is the 7._____

   A. names of the stations where the notices were posted
   B. time of day when the notices were posted
   C. date when the notices were posted
   D. name and pass number of the assistant station supervisor posting the notices

8. If loose notices without notations on them are found, the situation should be investigated to make sure that the 8._____

   A. notices are properly returned to the Station Department
   B. assistant station supervisor responsible for the error is found
   C. notices are correct for the diversion involved
   D. notices have been distributed properly

9. To insure that employees are aware of a diversion in service, an assistant station supervisor covering the group and hour when a diversion exists must contact the involved stations 9._____

   A. immediately after the diversion
   B. on an hourly basis
   C. on a daily basis
   D. as often as possible

10. To make certain affected stations have notices posted when diversions occur, spot checks should be made by 10._____

    A. station supervisors daily
    B. station supervisors when necessary
    C. assistant station supervisors daily
    D. assistant station supervisors when necessary

Questions 11-15.

DIRECTIONS: Questions 11 through 15 are to be answered on the basis of the following paragraph entitled PROCEDURE FOR FLAGGING DISABLED TRAIN.

PROCEDURE FOR FLAGGING DISABLED TRAIN

If at any time it becomes necessary to operate a train from other than the forward cab of the leading car, a qualified Rapid Transit Transportation Department employee must be stationed on the forward end. The motorman and the aforesaid qualified employee must have a clear understanding as to the signals to be used between them as well as to the method of operation. They must know, by actual test, that they have communication between them. Flagging signals should be given at short intervals while train is in motion. If train is carrying passengers, they must be discharged at the next station. Motormen operating from other than the forward cab of the leading car must not advance the controller beyond the *series position*.

11. The qualified employee stationed at the forward end must NOT be a 11._____

    A. motorman   B. conductor
    C. motorman instructor   D. road car inspector

12. While the train is in motion, the employees stationed at the forward end should give a flagging signal   12.____

    A. at frequent intervals
    B. every time the train is about to pass a fixed signal
    C. only when he wants the train speed changed
    D. only when he wants to check his understanding with the motorman

13. Motormen operating from other than the leading car must NOT advance the controller beyond   13.____

    A. switching   B. series   C. multiple   D. parallel

14. Considering the actual conditions on a passenger train in the subway, the MOST practical method of communication between the motorman and the employee at the forward end would be by using the   14.____

    A. train public address system   B. buzzer signals
    C. whistle signals   D. lantern signals

15. The BEST reason for discharging passengers at the next station under these conditions is that   15.____

    A. carrying passengers would cause additional delays
    B. it is not possible to operate safely
    C. the motorman cannot see the station stop markers
    D. the four lights at the front of the train will be red

Questions 16-25.

DIRECTIONS: Questions 16 through 25, inclusive, are based on the description given in the following special assignment for a group of cleaners. Read the description carefully before answering these questions. Be sure to consider ONLY the information contained in these paragraphs.

SPECIAL ASSIGNMENT

A special assignment of washing the ceilings and the tile walls of a number of stations on a particular line was given to a group of railroad cleaners. The stations included in the assignment were both local and express stations, and the only means of transferring between the uptown and the downtown trains without going to the street was to be found at the express stations. The stations to be cleaned were 2nd Street, 9th Street, 16th Street, 22nd Street, 29th Street, 36th Street, 44th Street, 52nd Street, 60th Street, and 69th Street. Of these, the express stations were located at 16th Street, 44th Street, and 69th Street.

Only the uptown sides of the stations were to be cleaned, as another gang was to clean the downtown sides. The cleaning operations were to start at 2nd Street and progress uptown. The materials furnished to perform this work consisted of pails, soap, long-handled brushes, mops, rags, and canvas covers for scales and vending machines.

The instructions were to scrub a surface first with a brush that had been immersed in a pail of soapy water, and then follow up by brushing with clear water. Any equipment on stations that was left uncovered and was splashed in the cleaning process was to be wiped clean with a rag.

16. The total number of different kinds of materials furnished to do the work of the special 16.____
    assignment was

    A. 5   B. 6   C. 7   D. 8

17. Benches on station platforms were to be 17.____

    A. moved out of the work area
    B. covered with canvas
    C. wiped clean with a rag if splashed
    D. rinsed with clear water

18. Of the materials furnished, the instructions did NOT definitely call for the use of 18.____

    A. mops   B. brushes   C. pails   D. rags

19. The FIRST operation cleaners were instructed to do was to 19.____

    A. clean walls with scouring cleanser
    B. scrub ceilings with clear water
    C. wipe vending machines clean with rags
    D. scrub surfaces with soapy water

20. Furnished materials that were NOT used in the washing of ceilings included 20.____

    A. soap   B. pails   C. rags   D. water

21. Long-handled brushes were probably furnished because 21.____

    A. ladders cannot be used on stations
    B. such brushes are easier to handle than ordinary brushes
    C. a better job can be done, since both hands are used
    D. some areas could not be reached otherwise

22. Of the total number of stations included in the assignment, the number which were 22.____
    express stations was

    A. 3   B. 7   C. 10   D. 20

23. A cleaner working in the *uptown* gang at 52nd Street Station was sent by his supervisor to 23.____
    get some supplies from the *downtown* gang which happened to be working at the same
    station.
    The cleaner would have displayed good judgment if he

    A. boarded a downtown train to 44th Street, crossed over, and then boarded an
       uptown train
    B. descended to the tracks and crossed over cautiously
    C. boarded an uptown train to 69th Street, crossed over, and then boarded a down-
       town train
    D. went directly up to the street and crossed over

24. After finishing the assigned work at 44th Street, the men on this assignment were scheduled to go next to _____ Street.

   A. 16th   B. 36th   C. 52nd   D. 69th

25. A passenger at 29th Street wishing to transfer from a downtown local to an uptown local without paying an additional fare should transfer at _____ Street.

   A. 44th   B. 16th   C. 36th   D. 22nd

KEY (CORRECT ANSWERS)

1. B		11. D	
2. C		12. A	
3. D		13. B	
4. C		14. B	
5. A		15. A	
6. B		16. B	
7. B		17. C	
8. D		18. A	
9. C		19. D	
10. A		20. C	

21. D
22. A
23. D
24. C
25. B

READING COMPREHENSION
UNDERSTANDING AND INTERPRETING WRITTEN MATERIAL
EXAMINATION SECTION
TEST 1

DIRECTIONS: Each question or incomplete statement is followed by several suggested answers or completions. Select the one that BEST answers the question or completes the statement. *PRINT THE LETTER OF THE CORRECT ANSWER IN THE SPACE AT THE RIGHT.*

Questions 1-8.

DIRECTIONS: Questions 1 through 8 are to be answered on the basis of the following regulations governing Newspaper Carriers when on subway trains or station platforms. These Newspaper Carriers are issued badges which entitle them to enter subway stations, when carrying papers in accordance with these regulations, without paying a fare.

REGULATIONS GOVERNING NEWSPAPER CARRIERS WHEN ON SUBWAY TRAINS OR STATION PLATFORMS

1. Carriers must wear badges at all times when on trains.
2. Carriers must not sort, separate, or wrap bundles on trains or insert sections.
3. Carriers must not obstruct platform of cars or stations.
4. Carriers may make delivery to stands inside the stations by depositing their badge with the station agent.
5. Throwing of bundles is strictly prohibited and will be cause for arrest.
6. Each bundle must not be over 18" x 12" x 15".
7. Not more than two bundles shall be carried by each carrier. (An extra fare to be charged for a second bundle.)
8. No wire to be used on bundles carried into stations.

1. These regulations do NOT prohibit carriers on trains from _____ newspapers. 1._____

    A. sorting bundles of B. carrying bundles of
    C. wrapping bundles of D. inserting sections into

2. A carrier delivering newspapers to a stand inside of the station MUST 2._____

    A. wear his badge at all times
    B. leave his badge with the railroad clerk
    C. show his badge to the railroad clerk
    D. show his badge at the newsstand

3. Carriers are warned against throwing bundles of newspapers from trains MAINLY because these acts may 3._____

    A. wreck the stand B. cause injury to passengers
    C. hurt the carrier D. damage the newspaper

4. It is permissible for a carrier to temporarily leave his bundles of newspapers

   A. near the subway car's door
   B. at the foot of the station stairs
   C. in front of the exit gate
   D. on a station bench

5. Of the following, the carrier who should NOT be restricted from entering the subway is the one carrying a bundle which is _____ long, _____ wide, and _____ high.

   A. 15"; 18"; 18"
   B. 18"; 12"; 18"
   C. 18"; 12"; 15"
   D. 18"; 15"; 15"

6. A carrier who will have to pay one fare is carrying _____ bundle(s).

   A. one   B. two   C. three   D. four

7. Wire may NOT be used for tying bundles because it may be

   A. rusty
   B. expensive
   C. needed for other purposes
   D. dangerous to other passengers

8. If a carrier is arrested in violation of these regulations, the PROBABLE reason is that he

   A. carried too many papers
   B. was not wearing his badge
   C. separated bundles of newspapers on the train
   D. tossed a bundle of newspapers to a carrier on a train

Questions 9-12.

DIRECTIONS: Questions 9 through 12 are to be answered on the basis of the Bulletin printed below. Read this Bulletin carefully before answering these questions. Select your answers ONLY on the basis of this Bulletin.

BULLETIN

Rule 107(m) states, in part, that *Before closing doors they (Conductors) must afford passengers an opportunity to detrain and entrain...*

Doors must be left open long enough to allow passengers to enter and exit from the train. Closing doors on passengers too quickly does not help to shorten the station stop and is a violation of the safety and courtesy which must be accorded to all our passengers.

The proper and effective way to keep passengers moving in and out of the train is to use the public address system. When the train is excessively crowded and passengers on the platform are pushing those in the cars, it may be necessary to close the doors after a reasonable period of time has been allowed.

Closing doors on passengers too quickly is a violation of rules and will be cause for disciplinary actions.

9. Which of the following statements is CORRECT about closing doors on passengers too quickly? It

   A. will shorten the running time from terminal to terminal
   B. shortens the station stop but is a violation of safety and courtesy
   C. does not help shorten the station stop time
   D. makes the passengers detrain and entrain quicker

9._____

10. The BEST way to get passengers to move in and out of cars quickly is to

    A. have the platform conductors urge passengers to move into doorways
    B. make announcements over the public address system
    C. start closing doors while passengers are getting on
    D. set a fixed time for stopping at each station

10._____

11. The conductor should leave doors open at each station stop long enough for passengers to

    A. squeeze into an excessively crowded train
    B. get from the local to the express train
    C. get off and get on the train
    D. hear the announcements over the public address system

11._____

12. Closing doors on passengers too quickly is a violation of rules and is cause for

    A. the conductor's immediate suspension
    B. the conductor to be sent back to the terminal for another assignment
    C. removal of the conductor at the next station
    D. disciplinary action to be taken against the conductor

12._____

Questions 13-15.

DIRECTIONS: Questions 13 through 15 are to be answered on the basis of the Bulletin printed below. Read this Bulletin carefully before answering these questions. Select your answers ONLY on the basis of this Bulletin.

BULLETIN

Conductors assigned to train service are not required to wear uniform caps from June 1 to September 30, inclusive.

Conductors assigned to platform duty are required to wear the uniform cap at all times. Conductors are reminded that they must furnish their badge numbers to anyone who requests same.

During the above-mentioned period, conductors may remove their uniform coats. The regulation summer short-sleeved shirts must be worn with the regulation uniform trousers. Suspenders are not permitted if the uniform coat is removed. Shoes are to be black but sandals, sneakers, suede, canvas, or two-tone footwear must not be worn.

Conductors may work without uniform tie if the uniform coat is removed. However, only the top collar button may be opened. The tie may not be removed if the uniform coat is worn.

13. Conductors assigned to platform duty are required to wear uniform caps

    A. at all times except from June 1 to September 30, inclusive
    B. whenever they are on duty
    C. only from June 1 to September 30, inclusive
    D. only when they remove their uniform coats

14. Suspenders are permitted ONLY if conductors wear

    A. summer short-sleeved shirts with uniform trousers
    B. uniform trousers without belt loops
    C. the type permitted by the authority
    D. uniform coats

15. A conductor MUST furnish his badge number to

    A. authority supervisors only
    B. members of special inspection only
    C. anyone who asks him for it
    D. passengers only

Questions 16-17.

DIRECTIONS: Questions 16 and 17 are to be answered SOLELY on the basis of the following Bulletin.

BULLETIN

Effective immediately, Conductors on trains equipped with public address systems shall make the following announcements in addition to their regular station announcement. At stations where passengers normally board trains from their homes or places of employment, the announcement shall be *Good Morning* or *Good Afternoon* or *Good Evening*, depending on the time of the day. At stations where passengers normally leave trains for their homes or places of employment, the announcement shall be *Have a Good Day* or *Good Night*, depending on the time of day or night.

16. The MAIN purpose of making the additional announcements mentioned in the Bulletin is MOST likely to

    A. keep passengers informed about the time of day
    B. determine whether the public address system works in case of an emergency
    C. make the passengers' ride more pleasant
    D. have the conductor get used to using the public address system

17. According to this Bulletin, a conductor should greet passengers boarding the *D* train at the Coney Island Station at 8 A.M. Monday by announcing

    A. Have a Good Day
    B. Good Morning
    C. Watch your step as you leave
    D. Good Evening

Questions 18-25.

DIRECTIONS: Questions 18 through 25 are to be answered on the basis of the information regarding the incident given below. Read this information carefully before answering these questions.

INCIDENT

As John Brown, a cleaner, was sweeping the subway station platform, in accordance with his assigned schedule, he was accused by Henry Adams of unnecessarily bumping him with the broom and scolded for doing this work when so many passengers were on the platform. Adams obtained Brown's badge number and stated that he would report the matter to the Transit Authority. Standing around and watching this were Mary Smith, a schoolteacher, Ann Jones, a student, and Joe Black, a maintainer, with Jim Roe, his helper, who had been working on one of the turnstiles. Brown thereupon proceeded to take the names and addresses of these people as required by the Transit Authority rule which directs that names and addresses of as many disinterested witnesses be taken as possible. Shortly thereafter, a train arrived at the station and Adams, as well as several other people, boarded the train and left. Brown went back to his work of sweeping the station.

18. The cleaner was sweeping the station at this time because

    A. the platform was unusually dirty
    B. there were very few passengers on the platform
    C. he had no regard for the passengers
    D. it was set by his work schedule

19. This incident proves that

    A. witnesses are needed in such cases
    B. porters are generally careless
    C. subway employees stick together
    D. brooms are dangerous in the subway

20. Joe Black was a

    A. helper   B. maintainer
    C. cleaner   D. teacher

21. The number of persons witnessing this incident was

    A. 2   B. 3   C. 4   D. 5

22. The addresses of witnesses are required so that they may later be

    A. depended on to testify   B. recognized
    C. paid   D. located

23. The person who said he would report this incident to the transit authority was

    A. Black   B. Adams   C. Brown   D. Roe

24. The ONLY person of the following who positively did NOT board the train was
    A. Brown   B. Smith   C. Adams   D. Jones

25. As a result of this incident,
    A. no action need be taken against the cleaner unless Adams makes a written complaint
    B. the cleaner should be given the rest of the day off
    C. the handles of the brooms used should be made shorter
    D. Brown's badge number should be changed

KEY (CORRECT ANSWERS)

1.	B	11.	C
2.	B	12.	D
3.	B	13.	B
4.	D	14.	D
5.	C	15.	C
6.	A	16.	C
7.	D	17.	B
8.	D	18.	D
9.	C	19.	A
10.	B	20.	B

21. C
22. D
23. B
24. A
25. A

TEST 2

DIRECTIONS: Each question or incomplete statement is followed by several suggested answers or completions. Select the one that BEST answers the question or completes the statement. *PRINT THE LETTER OF THE CORRECT ANSWER IN THE SPACE AT THE RIGHT.*

Questions 1-10.

DIRECTIONS: Questions 1 through 10 are to be answered on the basis of the information contained in the following safety rules. Read the rules carefully before answering these questions.

SAFETY RULES

Employees must take every precaution to prevent accidents, or injury to persons, or damage to property. For this reason, they must observe conditions of the equipment and tools with which they work, and the structures upon which they work.

It is the duty of all employees to report to their superior all dangerous conditions which they may observe. Employees must use every precaution to prevent the origin of fire. If they discover smoke or a fire in the subway, they shall proceed to the nearest telephone and notify the trainmaster giving their name, badge number, and location of the trouble.

In case of accidents on the subway system, employees must, if possible, secure the name, address, and telephone number of any passengers who may have been injured.

Employees at or near the location of trouble on the subway system, whether it be a fire or an accident, shall render all practical assistance which they are qualified to perform.

1. The BEST way for employees to prevent an accident is to

   A. secure the names of the injured persons
   B. arrive promptly at the location of the accident
   C. give their name and badge numbers to the trainmaster
   D. take all necessary precautions

2. In case of trouble, trackmen are NOT expected to

   A. report fires
   B. give help if they don't know how
   C. secure telephone numbers of persons injured in subway accidents
   D. give their badge number to anyone

3. Trackmen MUST

   A. be present at all fires
   B. see all accidents
   C. report dangerous conditions
   D. be the first to discover smoke in the subway

4. Observing conditions means to

   A. look at things carefully
   B. report what you see
   C. ignore things that are none of your business
   D. correct dangerous conditions

5. A dangerous condition existing on the subway system which a trackman should observe and report to his superior would be

   A. passengers crowding into trains
   B. trains running behind schedule
   C. tools in defective condition
   D. some newspapers on the track

6. If a trackman discovers a badly worn rail, he should

   A. not take any action
   B. remove the worn section of rail
   C. notify his superior
   D. replace the rail

7. The MAIN reason a trackman should observe the condition of his tools is

   A. so that they won't be stolen
   B. because they don't belong to him
   C. to prevent accidents
   D. because they cannot be replaced

8. If a passenger who paid his fare is injured in a subway accident, it is MOST important that an employee obtain the passenger's

   A. name
   B. age
   C. badge number
   D. destination

9. An employee who happens to be at the scene of an accident on a crowded station of the system should

   A. not give assistance unless he chooses to do so
   B. leave the scene immediately
   C. question all bystanders
   D. render whatever assistance he can

10. If a trackman discovers a fire at one end of a station platform and telephones the information to the trainmaster, he need NOT give

    A. the trainmaster's name
    B. the name of the station involved
    C. his own name
    D. the number of his badge

Questions 11-15.

DIRECTIONS: Questions 11 through 15 are to be answered on the basis of the information contained in the safety regulations given below. Refer to these rules in answering these questions.

REGULATIONS FOR SMALL GROUPS WHO MOVE FROM POINT TO POINT ON THE TRACKS

Employees who perform duties on the tracks in small groups and who move from point to point along the trainway must be on the alert at all times and prepared to clear the track when a train approaches without unnecessarily slowing it down. Underground at all times, and out-of-doors between sunset and sunrise, such employees must not enter upon the tracks unless each of them is equipped with an approved light. Flashlights must not be used for protection by such groups. Upon clearing the track to permit a train to pass, each member of the group must give a proceed signal, by hand or light, to the motorman of the train. Whenever such small groups are working in an area protected by caution lights or flags, but are not members of the gang for whom the flagging protection was established, they must not give proceed signals to motormen. The purpose of this rule is to avoid a motorman's confusing such signal with that of the flagman who is protecting a gang. Whenever a small group is engaged in work of an engrossing nature or at any time when the view of approaching trains is limited by reason of curves or otherwise, one man of the group, equipped with a whistle, must be assigned properly to warn and protect the man or men at work and must not perform any other duties while so assigned.

11. If a small group of men are traveling along the tracks toward their work location and a train approaches, they should

    A. stop the train
    B. signal the motorman to go slowly
    C. clear the track
    D. stop immediately

12. Small groups may enter upon the tracks

    A. only between sunset and sunrise
    B. provided each has an approved light
    C. provided their foreman has a good flashlight
    D. provided each man has an approved flashlight

13. After a small group has cleared the tracks in an area unprotected by caution lights or flags,

    A. each member must give the proceed signal to the motorman
    B. the foreman signals the motorman to proceed
    C. the motorman can proceed provided he goes slowly
    D. the last member off the tracks gives the signal to the motorman

14. If a small group is working in an area protected by the signals of a track gang, the members of the small group

    A. need not be concerned with train movement
    B. must give the proceed signal together with the track gang

C. can delegate one of their members to give the proceed signal
D. must not give the proceed signal

15. If the view of approaching trains is blocked, the small group should

    A. move to where they can see the trains
    B. delegate one of the group to warn and protect them
    C. keep their ears alert for approaching trains
    D. refuse to work at such locations

Questions 16-25.

DIRECTIONS: Questions 16 through 25 are to be answered SOLELY on the basis of the article about general safety precautions given below.

GENERAL SAFETY PRECAUTIONS

When work is being done on or next to a track on which regular trains are running, special signals must be displayed as called for in the general rules for flagging. Yellow caution signals, green clear signals, and a flagman with a red danger signal are required for the protection of traffic and workmen in accordance with the standard flagging rules. The flagman shall also carry a white signal for display to the motorman when he may proceed. The foreman in charge must see that proper signals are displayed.

On elevated lines during daylight hours, the yellow signal shall be a yellow flag, the red signal shall be a red flag, the green signal shall be a green flag, and the white signal shall be a white flag. In subway sections, and on elevated lines after dark, the yellow signal shall be a yellow lantern, the red signal shall be a red lantern, the green signal shall be a green lantern, and the white signal shall be a white lantern.

Caution and clear signals are to be secured to the elevated or subway structure with non-metallic fastenings outside the clearance line of the train and on the motorman's side of the track.

16. On elevated lines during daylight hours, the caution signal is a

    A. yellow lantern   B. green lantern
    C. yellow flag   D. green flag

17. In subway sections, the clear signal is a

    A. yellow lantern   B. green lantern
    C. yellow flag   D. green flag

18. The MINIMUM number of lanterns that a subway track flagman should carry is

    A. 1   B. 2   C. 3   D. 4

19. The PRIMARY purpose of flagging is to protect the

    A. flagman   B. motorman
    C. track workers   D. railroad

20. A suitable fastening for securing caution lights to the elevated or subway structure is 20._____

  A. copper nails B. steel wire
  C. brass rods D. cotton twine

21. On elevated structures during daylight hours, the red flag is held by the 21._____

  A. motorman B. foreman C. trackman D. flagman

22. The signal used in the subway to notify a motorman to proceed is a 22._____

  A. white lantern B. green lantern
  C. red flag D. yellow flag

23. The caution, clear, and danger signals are displayed for the information of 23._____

  A. trackmen B. workmen C. flagmen D. motormen

24. Since the motorman's cab is on the right-hand side, caution signals should be secured to the 24._____

  A. right-hand running rail
  B. left-hand running rail
  C. structure to the right of the track
  D. structure to the left of the track

25. In a track work gang, the person responsible for the proper display of signals is the 25._____

  A. track worker B. foreman
  C. motorman D. flagman

KEY (CORRECT ANSWERS)

1.	D	11.	C
2.	B	12.	B
3.	C	13.	A
4.	A	14.	D
5.	C	15.	B
6.	C	16.	C
7.	C	17.	B
8.	A	18.	B
9.	D	19.	C
10.	A	20.	D

21. D
22. A
23. D
24. C
25. B

TEST 3

DIRECTIONS: Each question or incomplete statement is followed by several suggested answers or completions. Select the one that BEST answers the question or completes the statement. *PRINT THE LETTER OF THE CORRECT ANSWER IN THE SPACE AT THE RIGHT.*

Questions 1-6.

DIRECTIONS: Questions 1 through 6 are to be answered on the basis of the Bulletin Order given below. Refer to this bulletin when answering these questions.

BULLETIN ORDER NO. 67

SUBJECT: Procedure for Handling Fire Occurrences

In order that the Fire Department may be notified of all fires, even those that have been extinguished by our own employees, any employee having knowledge of a fire must notify the Station Department Office immediately on telephone extensions D-4177, D-4181, D-4185, or D-4189.

Specific information regarding the fire should include the location of the fire, the approximate distance north or south of the nearest station, and the track designation, line, and division.

In addition, the report should contain information as to the status of the fire and whether our forces have extinguished it or if Fire Department equipment is required.

When all information has been obtained, the Station Supervisor in Charge in the Station Department Office will notify the Desk Trainmaster of the Division involved.

Richard Roe,
Superintendent

1. An employee having knowledge of a fire should FIRST notify the

   A. Station Department Office
   B. Fire Department
   C. Desk Trainmaster
   D. Station Supervisor

1._____

2. If bulletin order number 1 was issued on January 2, bulletins are being issued at the monthly average of

   A. 8   B. 10   C. 12   D. 14

2._____

3. It is clear from the bulletin that

   A. employees are expected to be expert fire fighters
   B. many fires occur on the transit system
   C. train service is usually suspended whenever a fire occurs
   D. some fires are extinguished without the help of the Fire Department

3._____

4. From the information furnished in this bulletin, it can be assumed that the

   A. Station Department office handles a considerable number of telephone calls
   B. Superintendent Investigates the handling of all subway fires
   C. Fire Department is notified only in ease of large fires
   D. employee first having knowledge of the fire must call all 4 extensions

5. The PROBABLE reason for notifying the Fire Department even when the fire has been extinguished by a subway employee is because the Fire Department is

   A. a city agency
   B. still responsible to check the fire
   C. concerned with fire prevention
   D. required to clean up after the fire

6. Information about the fire NOT specifically required is

   A. track   B. time of day   C. station   D. division

Questions 7-10.

DIRECTIONS: Questions 7 through 10 are to be answered on the basis of the paragraph on fire fighting shown below. When answering these questions, refer to this paragraph.

FIRE FIGHTING

A security officer should remember the cardinal rule that water or soda acid fire extinguishers should not be used on any electrical fire, and apply it in the case of a fire near the third rail. In addition, security officers should familiarize themselves with all available fire alarms and fire-fighting equipment within their assigned posts. Use of the fire alarm should bring responding Fire Department apparatus quickly to the scene. Familiarity with the fire-fighting equipment near his post would help in putting out incipient fires. Any man calling for the Fire Department should remain outside so that he can direct the Fire Department to the fire. As soon as possible thereafter, the special inspection desk must be notified, and a complete written report of the fire, no matter how small, must be submitted to this office. The security officer must give the exact time and place it started, who discovered it, how it was extinguished, the damage done, cause of same, list of any injured persons with the extent of their injuries, and the name of the Fire Chief in charge. All defects noticed by the security officer concerning the fire alarm or any fire-fighting equipment must be reported to the special inspection department.

7. It would be PROPER to use water to put out a fire in a(n)

   A. electric motor   B. electric switch box
   C. waste paper trash can   D. electric generator

8. After calling the Fire Department from a street box to report a fire, the security officer should then

   A. return to the fire and help put it out
   B. stay outside and direct the Fire Department to the fire
   C. find a phone and call his boss
   D. write out a report for the special inspection desk

9. A security officer is required to submit a complete written report of a fire

   A. two weeks after the fire
   B. the day following the fire
   C. as soon as possible
   D. at his convenience

10. In his report of a fire, it is NOT necessary for the security officer to state

    A. time and place of the fire
    B. who discovered the fire
    C. the names of persons injured
    D. quantity of Fire Department equipment used

Questions 11-16.

DIRECTIONS: Questions 11 through 16 are to be answered on the basis of the Notice given below. Refer to this Notice in answering these questions.

NOTICE

Your attention is called to Route Request Buttons that are installed on all new type Interlocking Home Signals where there is a choice of route in the midtown area. The route request button is to be operated by the motorman when the home signal is at danger and no call-on is displayed or when improper route is displayed.

To operate, the motorman will press the button for the desiredroute as indicated under each button; a light will then go on over the buttons to inform the motorman that his request has been registered in the tower.

If the towerman desires to give the motorman a route other than the one he selected, the towerman will cancel out the light over the route selection buttons. The motorman will then accept the route given.

If no route or call-on is given, the motorman will sound his whistle for the signal maintainer, secure his train, and call the desk trainmaster.

11. The official titles of the two classes of employee whose actions would MOST frequently be affected by the contents of this notice are

    A. motorman and trainmaster
    B. signal maintainer and trainmaster
    C. towerman and motorman
    D. signal maintainer and towerman

12. A motorman should use a route request button when

    A. the signal indicates proceed on main line
    B. a call-on is displayed
    C. the signal indicates stop
    D. the signal indicates proceed on diverging route

13. The PROPER way to request a route is to 13.____
    A. press the button corresponding to the desired route
    B. press the button a number of times to correspond with the number of the route requested
    C. stop at the signal and blow four short blasts
    D. stop at the signal and telephone the tower

14. The motorman will know that his requested route has been registered in the tower if 14.____
    A. a light comes on over the route request buttons
    B. an acknowledging signal is sounded on the tower horn
    C. the light in the route request button goes dark
    D. the home signal continues to indicate stop

15. Under certain conditions, when stopped at such home signal, the motorman must signal for a signal maintainer and call the desk trainmaster. 15.____
    Such condition exists when, after standing awhile,
    A. the towerman continues to give the wrong route
    B. the towerman does not acknowledge the signal
    C. no route or call-on is given
    D. the light over the route request buttons is cancelled out

16. It is clear that route request buttons 16.____
    A. eliminate train delays due to signals at junctions
    B. keep the towerman alert
    C. force motormen and towermen to be more careful
    D. are a more accurate form of communication than the whistle.

Questions 17-22.

DIRECTIONS: Questions 17 through 22 are to be answered on the basis of the instructions for removal of paper given below. Read these instructions carefully before answering these questions.

GENERAL INSTRUCTIONS FOR REMOVAL OF PAPER

When a cleaner's work schedule calls for the bagging of paper, he will remove paper from the waste paper receptacles, bag it, and place the bags at the head end of the platform, where they will be picked up by the work train. He will fill bags with paper to a weight that can be carried without danger of personal injury, as porters are forbidden to drag bags of paper over the platform. Cleaners are responsible that all bags of paper are arranged so as to prevent their falling from the platform to tracks, and so as to not interfere with passenger traffic.

17. A GOOD reason for removing the paper from receptacles and placing it in bags is that bags are more easily 17.____

    A. stored   B. weighed   C. handled   D. emptied

18. The *head end* of a local station platform is the end 18.___

    A. in the direction that trains are running
    B. nearest to which the trains stop
    C. where there is an underpass to the other side
    D. at which the change booth is located

19. The MOST likely reason for having the filled bags placed at the head end of the station rather than at the other end is that 19.___

    A. a special storage space is provided there for them
    B. this end of the platform is farthest from the passengers
    C. most porters' closets are located near the head end
    D. the work train stops at this end to pick them up

20. Limiting the weight to which the bags can be filled is PROBABLY done to 20.___

    A. avoid having too many ripped or broken bags
    B. protect the porter against possible rupture
    C. make sure that all bags are filled fairly evenly
    D. insure that, when stored, the bags will not fall to the track

21. The MOST important reason for not allowing filled bags to be dragged over the platform is that the bags 21.___

    A. could otherwise be loaded too heavily
    B. might leave streaks on the platform
    C. would wear out too quickly
    D. might spill paper on the platform

22. The instructions do NOT hold a porter responsible for a bag of paper which 22.___

    A. is torn due to dragging over a platform
    B. falls on a passenger because it was poorly stacked
    C. falls to the track without being pushed
    D. is ripped open by school children

Questions 23-25.

DIRECTIONS: Questions 23 through 25 are to be answered on the basis of the situation described below. Consider the facts given in this situation when answering these questions.

SITUATION

A new detergent that is to be added to water and the resulting mixture just wiped on any surface has been tested by the station department and appeared to be excellent. However, you notice, after inspecting a large number of stations that your porters have cleaned with this detergent, that the surfaces cleaned are not as clean as they formerly were when the old method was used.

ANSWER SHEET

TEST NO. _____ PART _____ TITLE OF POSITION _____
(AS GIVEN IN EXAMINATION ANNOUNCEMENT - INCLUDE OPTION, IF ANY)

PLACE OF EXAMINATION _____ DATE _____
(CITY OR TOWN)   (STATE)

RATING

USE THE SPECIAL PENCIL. MAKE GLOSSY BLACK MARKS.

Make only ONE mark for each answer. Additional and stray marks may be counted as mistakes. In making corrections, erase errors COMPLETELY.

ANSWER SHEET

TEST NO. _____ PART _____ TITLE OF POSITION _____
(AS GIVEN IN EXAMINATION ANNOUNCEMENT - INCLUDE OPTION, IF ANY)

PLACE OF EXAMINATION _____ DATE _____
(CITY OR TOWN)   (STATE)

RATING

USE THE SPECIAL PENCIL.   MAKE GLOSSY BLACK MARKS.

Make only ONE mark for each answer. Additional and stray marks may be counted as mistakes. In making corrections, erase errors COMPLETELY.

23. The MAIN reason for the station department testing the new detergent in the first place was to make certain that 23.____

    A. it was very simple to use
    B. a little bit would go a long way
    C. there was no stronger detergent on the market
    D. it was superior to anything formerly used

24. The MAIN reason that such a poor cleaning job resulted was MOST likely due to the 24.____

    A. porters being lax on the job
    B. detergent not being as good as expected
    C. incorrect amount of water being mixed with the detergent
    D. fact that the surfaces cleaned needed to be scrubbed

25. The reason for inspecting a number of stations was to 25.____

    A. determine whether all porters did the same job
    B. insure that the result of the cleaning job was the same in each location
    C. be certain that the detergent was used in each station inspected
    D. see whether certain surfaces cleaned better than others

---

KEY (CORRECT ANSWERS)

1.	A	11.	C
2.	C	12.	C
3.	D	13.	A
4.	A	14.	A
5.	C	15.	C
6.	B	16.	D
7.	C	17.	C
8.	B	18.	A
9.	C	19.	D
10.	D	20.	B

21. C
22. D
23. D
24. B
25. B
